OUR GREAT SALVATION

LIGONIER MINISTRIES

OUR
GREAT
SALVATION

A
90
DAY DEVOTIONAL

ON THE

CHRISTIAN LIFE

ORLANDO, FL

Our Great Salvation: A 90-Day Devotional on the Christian Life
© 2024 by Ligonier Ministries

Published by Ligonier Ministries
421 Ligonier Court, Sanford, FL 32771
Ligonier.org

Printed in Ann Arbor, Michigan
Cushing-Malloy, Inc.
0001223
First printing

ISBN 978-1-64289-550-6 (Paperback)
ISBN 978-1-64289-551-3 (ePub)

Cover design: Metaleap Creative
Interior typeset: Katherine Lloyd, The DESK

Devotions previously published in *Tabletalk* magazine.

Library of Congress Control Number: 2023938133

PREFACE

G od is the Giver of life. The opening pages of Scripture testify to His life-giving power, especially where we see Him breathe into Adam's nostrils the breath of life (Gen. 2:7). God created Adam and Eve to experience perfect life through their fellowship with Him and their submission to His benevolent rule. But Satan's temptation of Adam and Eve, which culminated in the fall of humankind, brought sin and death into God's good creation (Rom. 5:12).

God's provision of animal skins to cover Adam and Eve's nakedness after their sin reveals a truth that unfolds throughout Scripture: a sacrifice is required to restore what was lost in the fall. The Old Testament saints trusted in God's promises to send an ultimate Redeemer as they offered the sacrifices commanded by God, sacrifices that prefigured this ultimate sacrifice of God's own Son.

Despite Israel's failure to remain faithful to God's covenant, God remained faithful. At God's appointed time, the second person of the Trinity, Jesus Christ, took on human flesh, being born of a virgin, and walked upon the earth that He had created. Throughout His earthly ministry, Jesus made His identity clear: He Himself *is* life, and He came to lay down His life for God's people (John 14:6; 10:11). Jesus is not simply one path to life among other paths. He is the only path that leads to life; all other paths lead to death. Only by believing that He is the only perfect and final sacrifice to satisfy God's righteous demands can we have life (20:31).

When we place our trust in Christ alone as Savior, we pass from spiritual death to life (5:24). We are now united to Christ. We are *in* Christ. And so begins the Christian life.

STUDYING THE CHRISTIAN LIFE

The Christian life is not, therefore, seeking to live a moral life by our own efforts and in our own strength. The Christian life is not produced by church attendance, being a "good" person, or acquiring biblical knowledge. Rather, the Christian life is nothing less than the very life of the risen Christ at work in us through the Holy Spirit, enabling us to see and worship the glory and beauty of Christ, and empowering us to walk in His footsteps as we grow in love for the triune God and in love for others.

This is the Christian life that we will explore in this devotional— one in which God sovereignly brings His people from death to life by giving them new hearts, causing them to embrace the crucified and risen Jesus as the only hope for sinners and, in union with Him, to grow in closeness and conformity to Him, all to the praise of His glorious grace (Eph. 1:6).

HOW TO USE THIS DEVOTIONAL

This devotional has been designed to help believers understand some of the fundamental truths regarding the Christian life so that they may more fully live to the glory of God. Over the course of ninety days, you will explore different facets of the Christian life according to Scripture's teaching.

The devotional is divided into four sections: God, Salvation, Worship, and Sanctification. The first section covers who God is by exploring His triune nature and His attributes. The second section expands on understanding who God is by delving into His mighty works as the One who brings salvation. In response to this glorious God and His salvation, the third section turns to the topic of worship, addressing how believers are to respond to our gracious God. And finally, in the fourth section, we explore sanctification and what it means to grow closer to the Lord and become more like Him as we behold the glory of Christ.

Each devotional gives the passage of Scripture to be studied that day and highlights one or more of the most important verses from the passage for the subject of the study. Following the listed passage, you will find the body of the study, which will provide important background for the passage, an explanation of the text, and a discussion of how the passage relates to other texts of Scripture and theological concepts. The application section of each devotional provides practical considerations for daily life, and a list of other passages that have bearing on the study is also given. It is recommended that you read the Scripture passage for the day's study in its entirety before moving through the other sections of the devotional.

May these devotionals assist you in coming to a fuller knowledge of our great God and Savior. To Him alone be the glory forever.

I

GOD

Any consideration of the Christian life must start with considering God Himself. He is the Creator of all things. Yet only human beings are created in His image; therefore, human beings can relate to Him in a way that the rest of creation cannot (Gen. 1:27).

As finite creatures, we rely on our infinite Creator to reveal Himself to us. Psalm 19:1 and Romans 1:19-20 makes it plain that all humankind can perceive some of God's attributes through the world He has created. Further, God has put the basics of His moral law into human hearts through our consciences (Rom. 2:14-15).

Yet creation and conscience cannot reveal all that we must know about the eternal, triune God. And so God revealed Himself in human history through words, the Scriptures, to show us His character, purposes, and will. The supreme revelation of God occurred when the second person of the Trinity, Jesus Christ, took on human flesh and entered time and space in human history as the incarnate Word (John 1:1; Heb. 1:1-2).

So this triune God who is Creator and Redeemer is our beginning point as we consider the Christian life, for as Jesus Himself declared, "And this is eternal life, that they know you, the only true God, and Jesus Christ whom you have sent" (John 17:3).

THE ONE AND ONLY GOD

ISAIAH 45:5 "I AM THE LORD, AND THERE IS NO OTHER,
BESIDES ME THERE IS NO GOD; I EQUIP YOU, THOUGH YOU
DO NOT KNOW ME."

From the very beginning, Christianity has stood firmly upon the foundation of monotheism. Every part of Scripture, implicitly or explicitly, affirms that there is only one God, and belief in only one creator God is shared by many other non-Christian religions as well. But the monotheism taught by all Christian theological traditions, including Reformed theology, is different from the monotheism of religions such as Judaism and Islam because Christian monotheism is Trinitarian monotheism. Nevertheless, our doctrine of the Trinity is grounded in the foundational premise that there is but one eternal God who has created our universe.

Today's passage is one of many places that affirm this truth. Isaiah 45:5 firmly insists that the God revealed in Scripture is the only God. Note that when we speak of biblical monotheism, we are not speaking of deity in some generic sense. We are not talking about a vague concept of God that we arrive at via philosophical speculation, even though philosophy assists us in studying the doctrine of God. Instead, biblical monotheism proclaims that the only God is the One who redeemed Israel from Egyptian slavery and delivered His law through Moses. In Isaiah 45:5, two different Hebrew words for God appear. First, we have the word *elohim*, which is often used as a generic term for deity and is translated in our text as "God." Isaiah 45:5 also features the specific covenant name of the God of Israel—*Yahweh*—which is rendered in English as "LORD." Thus, we could paraphrase today's passage as "I, the LORD of Israel, am the only deity."

Yahweh is the only God regardless of whether we acknowledge Him as such. The addressee of Isaiah 45:5 is Cyrus of Persia (see vv. 1–4). Cyrus did not know God as He revealed

Himself—specifically, as the only true God. Yet that is irrelevant with respect to who God was in relation to Cyrus. Though Cyrus did not acknowledge Yahweh as such, He was Cyrus' God because Yahweh alone is God.

FOR FURTHER STUDY

Genesis 1:1; Deuteronomy 6:4; Romans 3:29; 1 Timothy 2:5

APPLICATION

It is not enough to believe in a generic God or to affirm any form of monotheism other than the monotheism of Scripture. There are many monotheists who will die in their sin because they believe in God but not in the true God, the covenant Lord of Israel. Salvation is only in His name, so when we proclaim the existence of God and defend it against detractors, let us be insistent that we are proclaiming that the one God is the God revealed in Scripture.

DAY 2

FALSE GODS

1 CHRONICLES 16:25-26 "GREAT IS THE Lord, AND GREATLY TO BE PRAISED, AND HE IS TO BE FEARED ABOVE ALL GODS. FOR ALL THE GODS OF THE PEOPLES ARE WORTHLESS IDOLS, BUT THE Lord MADE THE HEAVENS."

M onotheism, the conviction that there is only one God who has created the world, is fundamental to the Christian and Reformation doctrine of God. Furthermore, biblical monotheism asserts that the one creator God is not some generic deity but is rather Yahweh, the personal covenantal Lord of Israel (Isa. 45:5). Even though other religions such as Islam are monotheistic, the one god they worship is not the God proclaimed in Christian theology. Only that God, the God of the Bible, is God.

The fact that there is only one God, however, does not mean that the other beings called "gods" in Scripture are unreal. What does this mean? First, we have to note that many passages of Scripture seem to speak of gods as being nothing. Today's passage,

DAY 1 & 2

for example, says that "all the gods of the peoples are worthless idols" (1 Chron. 16:26). Paul explains in 1 Corinthians 8:4 that "an idol has no real existence." Yet these texts do not mean that there are not actual beings behind the idols or the deities we find in non-Christian religions. Instead, these passages mean that the other gods worshiped on this planet are not God in the true and proper sense. They are not the real God, the Creator who made all things. After all, "the LORD made the heavens" (1 Chron. 16:26), not any of the other beings worshiped in non-Christian religions. Those so-called gods are pretenders to the throne of the Almighty.

Second, the Bible reveals that while other gods are not God in a real sense, they do have a real existence as supernatural beings. "What pagans sacrifice they offer to demons and not to God" (1 Cor. 10:20). Biblical monotheism affirms the existence of a supernatural realm of angels, who serve God, and demons who are worshiped under such names as Krishna, Baal, and even Allah (when Muslims use the name). Yet the God of the Bible is not one among equals in this realm; rather, He stands outside and above it as its Creator, just as He stands outside and above the natural world. The Lord God of Israel is "most high over all the earth; . . . exalted far above all gods" (Ps. 97:9).

FOR FURTHER STUDY

2 Chronicles 2:5; Psalm 96:4; Isaiah 42:17; 1 Corinthians 12:2

These other "gods" exercise a tyrannical rule over their subjects, enslaving them to fear and uncertainty. If one does not serve the sovereign God over all, one cannot be sure that one's god can be of true help in a time of need. Another rival god might be stronger. But those who turn from the false gods to serve the one true God through Jesus Christ are released from such slavery (Gal. 4:8–9).

APPLICATION

As Christians, we should be the most courageous of peoples because we serve the one true God. We need not be afraid of what this world and the servants of other gods can do to us because they cannot win in the end. Those who are on the side of the one true God are secure in Him forever. Let us remember that we serve the only true God and need never fear the enemy.

GOD THE FATHER

EXODUS 4:22-23A "YOU SHALL SAY TO PHARAOH, 'THUS SAYS
THE LORD, ISRAEL IS MY FIRSTBORN SON, AND I SAY TO
YOU, "LET MY SON GO THAT HE MAY SERVE ME."'"

T he Protestant Reformers set out not to create a new religion but to bring the medieval Western church back to its biblical foundation. Proof of that can be seen in the fact that the Reformers left essentially unchanged the soundest biblical reflection from the fifteen hundred years of church history that preceded them. In other words, where the church had gotten things right biblically, they left things alone. We see this most fundamentally in the Reformation doctrine of God.

Reformation theologians affirmed the same biblical monotheism that was confessed by the Apostles and such figures as Athanasius, Augustine, and Thomas Aquinas. This means that the Reformers were Trinitarian in their view of God. Biblical monotheism is not unitarianism; it admits to particular distinctions within the Godhead. Though God is one in His essence, He is three in person—Father, Son, and Holy Spirit. Three coeternal, coequal persons share this essence in its entirety, possessing all the attributes that make God God.

We begin our look at the full deity of the three persons by considering the Father. That God is Father is revealed throughout Scripture. We see in today's passage, for example, that the Lord revealed Himself to Pharaoh as the Father of Israel (Ex. 4:22–23). It is the New Testament, however, that gives us a fuller picture of God as Father. Jesus, for example, frequently referred to the God of Israel as His Father (John 5:18). It is true that there is a way in which God is uniquely the Father of Jesus, yet Jesus' reference to God as Father goes beyond His unique relationship to God. Our Savior, after all, tells us to address God as "our Father" when we pray (Matt. 6:9–13). God stands in a fatherly relation to His people. More specifically, the first person of the Trinity, who is fully God, is our Father. Jesus, who is the incarnate Son and second person of the Trinity, is fully God and is our Brother (John 1:1; Heb. 2:11). The Holy Spirit, the third person of the Trinity, is fully God and is our Helper (John 14:26; Acts 5:3–4).

Importantly, the sovereign God of the universe is Father not to all people but only to those who trust in Jesus (John 1:12–13). The One who made all things takes us as His dearly beloved children in Christ. There is no better news than that.

FOR FURTHER STUDY

Isaiah 63:16; Jeremiah 3:4; John 4:21-24; 1 John 3:1a

APPLICATION

Good earthly fathers will do whatever is necessary to protect and provide for their sons and daughters. If that is true of our earthly fathers, how much more true is it of the Lord? Our Father who cares for us is omnipotent, and nothing can stand in the way of His providing for us. Let us thank Him this day for meeting all our needs, and let us trust that He will continue to do so.

DAY 4

GOD THE SON

JOHN 1:1-18 "IN THE BEGINNING WAS THE WORD, . . . AND THE WORD WAS GOD" (V. 1).

Biblical monotheism declares that God is one in essence and three in person. Among other things, this means that the Father, Son, and Holy Spirit are equally God, each possessing everything that is essential to deity.

Having considered the deity of the Father, we move today to considering the deity of the Son. John 1:1–18 contains some of the clearest teaching on this subject. In this text, we read of the Word of God who was God (v. 1) and of His incarnation (v. 14). This Word is also identified as the Son of God (v. 14), so we have in this passage John's presentation of God the Son, the second person of the Trinity, taking on a human nature and walking among us. Jesus Christ is the divine person of the Son of God in whom are perfectly and inseparably united deity and humanity, without mixture or confusion, with each nature retaining its own attributes.

Many other biblical texts present for us the deity of the Son of God. In addition to direct presentations of the full deity of Christ in passages such as John 1:1–18, we also find several other texts in which Christ does things that only God can do. Mark 2:1–12, for example, records our Savior as claiming the authority to forgive sins. The scribes understood exactly what He was doing, and they were offended. They would have been rightly offended if Jesus were not God incarnate. But though they were wrong about Jesus' identity, their offense demonstrates that they knew He was claiming deity for Himself.

There are other texts in which God's work is also attributed to Jesus. Jude 5, for instance, tells us that "Jesus, who saved a people out of the land of Egypt, afterward destroyed those who did not believe." Of course, the Old Testament attributes Israel's release from Egyptian slavery to Yahweh, the covenant Lord of Israel (Ex. 20:2), so Jude is telling us that Jesus is Yahweh. Jesus is the same God who rescued the Israelites from Pharaoh.

These texts are just the barest sample of the testimony of the New Testament to the deity of Christ. Only those with the hardest of hearts can deny that the Bible reveals Jesus as the Lord God Almighty who is worthy of all our love and worship.

FOR FURTHER STUDY

Isaiah 7:14;
Micah 5:2;
Romans 9:5;
2 Peter 1:1

APPLICATION

Jesus calls those who serve Him His friends (John 15:13–15), but this should not lead us to see Christ as merely a friend. The One who is our friend is also our Lord, and we are to seek to worship and honor Him in all that we do. To be a Christian is to worship Jesus as God.

DAY 5

THE FATHER AND THE SON

JOHN 1:1-18 "HE WAS IN THE BEGINNING WITH GOD" (V. 2).

Merely defending the deity of Christ is not enough to give us the biblical doctrine of God. More must be said about how Christ, who is God incarnate, is related to God the Father, who has not taken on flesh. John 1:1–18 not only demonstrates the deity of Christ but also proves His distinction from the Father. As we see in verses 1–2 of today's passage, the Word—the Son of God—in the beginning *was* God and *was with* God.

John introduces a distinction between God the Father and God the Son. Both are equally God, yet the Father is not the Son. Each possesses the full complement of divine attributes, but each in some way also has a particular identity. As John Calvin comments, "It would have been absurd in the Evangelist to say that the [Word] was always with God, if he had not some kind of subsistence peculiar to himself in God."

Over time, the church came to use the Greek word *hypostasis*, which we usually translate as "person," to refer to the distinctions within the one God. The Reformers adopted this terminology because it is a helpful way of describing the multiplicity that Scripture tells us belongs to the Godhead. The *hypostasis* of the Father is not the *hypostasis* of the Son, but both *hypostases* are *homoousios* (of the same essence).

This language is helpful, but we must note that it does not eliminate the mystery inherent to God. Our Creator is ultimately, but not totally, incomprehensible. We can know true things about Him, but we cannot know everything about Him. We cannot know Him as He knows Himself. It is difficult to define what we mean by *person* when we talk about the three persons of the Godhead, for in theological language, *person* is not identical to our modern concept of personhood. We are on safe ground to say little more than this: personhood in the Godhead means that while there is no difference among Father, Son, and Holy Spirit in terms of deity, there are still distinctions among the persons that enable Them to enjoy personal relations with one another, to love and be loved by the other persons.

FOR
FURTHER
STUDY
———
John 8:38;
Revelation
3:21

APPLICATION

In considering the biblical doctrine of Trinitarian monotheism, we will eventually reach a point where we can say no more. Because God transcends the limits of our creaturely minds, we cannot fully comprehend Him. This is a necessary facet of His greatness, and we should be overwhelmed by God's greatness whenever we think on the Trinity. Knowing the greatness of God will fuel our worship.

DAY 6

GOD THE HOLY SPIRIT

ACTS 5:1-11 "PETER SAID, 'ANANIAS, WHY HAS SATAN FILLED YOUR HEART TO LIE TO THE HOLY SPIRIT AND TO KEEP BACK FOR YOURSELF PART OF THE PROCEEDS OF THE LAND? WHILE IT REMAINED UNSOLD, DID IT NOT REMAIN YOUR OWN? AND AFTER IT WAS SOLD, WAS IT NOT AT YOUR DISPOSAL? WHY IS IT THAT YOU HAVE CONTRIVED THIS DEED IN YOUR HEART? YOU HAVE NOT LIED TO MAN BUT TO GOD'" (VV. 3-4).

According to Scripture, there is only one God. The one God is also three persons. John 1:1–18 helps us to understand this, describing the Son of God who at the same time *is* God and also is *with* God the Father. But Christian monotheism is Trinitarian and not binitarian, so it is now time for us to consider the third person of the Holy Trinity, God the Holy Spirit.

The Word of God teaches the full deity of the Holy Spirit in several places. Consider today's passage, which records the harsh judgment that Ananias and Sapphira received when they lied about a financial contribution they made to the church. In addressing Ananias, Peter said that he had lied "to the Holy Spirit" and that he had lied "to God" (Acts 5:3–4). Note how the terms "Holy Spirit" and "God" are used interchangeably. Clearly, this demonstrates that Peter believed the Holy Spirit to be the one God of Israel.

Second Peter 1:21 is also significant, for there Peter attributes the inspiration of the prophets to the Holy Spirit. But when we turn to the Old Testament Prophetic Books, we often find the prophets attributing their inspiration to Yahweh, the covenant Lord of Israel. For example, Hosea 1:1 says, "The word of the LORD that came to Hosea." Remember that "LORD" is a translation of God's covenant name, Yahweh. Thus, Peter says that the Yahweh who spoke by the prophets was the Holy Spirit. There is no difference in his mind between Yahweh and the Holy Spirit.

When we say that there is no difference between Yahweh and the Holy Spirit, we are speaking in terms of the divine essence, that which makes God who He is—namely, His divine moral character and His divine attributes. Within Yahweh, the one God and covenant Lord of Israel, there is a distinction between the Holy Spirit and the other two persons of the Trinity. The Holy Spirit is God, but He is not God the Son or God the Father. As proof of this, John 14:16 refers to the Holy Spirit as "another Helper." Here, the word "Helper" translates the Greek word *paraklēteos*, which in 1 John 2:1 is translated as "advocate" and is a title applied to "Jesus Christ the righteous." As Dr. R.C. Sproul has often noted, the Holy Spirit is not the only or even the first *paraklēteos* in Scripture; rather, God the Son, Jesus Christ, is the *paraklēteos* and the Holy Spirit is another *paraklēteos* alongside Him. The Spirit and the Son are one in essence, but They subsist distinctly within that essence.

FOR
FURTHER
STUDY

Genesis
1:1-2;
Psalm
104:27-30;
Matthew
28:18-20;
Acts 1:8

APPLICATION

Jesus no longer walks the earth in the flesh, but Scripture does not paint this as disadvantageous. Jesus has given us another Advocate or Helper like Himself. God incarnate has given us God the Holy Spirit (John 14:15–17), so our worship and service are animated by the very God of the universe. Thus, we can be confident that our worship and service have purpose and will accomplish what God intends for them.

DIVINE DIVERSITY

PSALM 110:1 "THE Lord SAYS TO MY LORD: 'SIT AT
MY RIGHT HAND, UNTIL I MAKE YOUR ENEMIES YOUR
FOOTSTOOL.'"

O ne of the oldest and most often-recurring heresies that has confronted the church is modalism. At its core, modalism is an error that denies the diversity within the Godhead. It collapses the distinctions between the three persons of the Godhead, proclaiming that the Father, Son, and Holy Spirit are identical both in essence and in person. In modalism, the Father, the Son, and the Holy Spirit do not exist from all eternity as persons that cannot be confused with one another. Instead, God is like one person who wears different masks or hats. Before the incarnation, the one God was Father. In the incarnation, God took off the Father hat and put on the Son hat. After the resurrection of Christ, God took off the Son hat and put on the Holy Spirit hat. From all eternity, the one God has existed not as three persons in perfect fellowship with one another but as one person in fellowship with no other person, for there was no other person before creation.

Scripture is quite clear, however, that the Godhead has possessed diversity from the beginning. In today's passage, we read about the Lord God's speaking to another Lord (Ps. 110:1). From Jesus' exposition of this passage in Matthew 22:41–46, we learn that the second Lord mentioned by David in the psalm, who is David's son, must also be greater than David. His words are an affirmation that the promised Messiah from David's line precedes and is greater than David's line. In other words, the Lord to whom David refers is both son of David and Son of God. Psalm 110:1 references the preexistence and deity of Christ. Yet in the same text we see a clear distinction between the two Lords mentioned. "The Lord" here speaks to a "Lord" who is the Son of God, and the fact that two Lords can speak to one another indicates the presence of two personal relations or subsistences, both of whom are

I

fully God. There is an eternal, personal distinction between God the Son and God the Father (but not in terms of Their essential attributes). In light of the full biblical witness, we may extrapolate this distinction to the person of the Holy Spirit as well, for Scripture in several places refers to all three persons in a manner that assumes distinctions between Them (see Matt. 28:18–20).

This eternal distinction between persons shows us that God is fundamentally personal. From all eternity, because God is three distinct persons, God has enjoyed personal relations. We worship not an impersonal force but a personal deity who relates to us intimately as creatures made in His image.

FOR FURTHER STUDY

Genesis 1:26a; 2 Corinthians 13:14; Galatians 4:6; Ephesians 1:2

APPLICATION

If God is an impersonal force, then we should pay Him little attention. We cannot know or relate to Him, and an impersonal being cannot be concerned with the affairs of human beings. But if God is a personal being, then we had better pay Him the closest attention of all. He is not unconcerned with us but pays heed to our every need, hope, and fear. We can bring everything before Him, knowing that He cares for His people.

DAY 8

DIVINE UNITY

MATTHEW 28:18-20 "GO THEREFORE AND MAKE DISCIPLES OF ALL NATIONS, BAPTIZING THEM IN THE NAME OF THE FATHER AND OF THE SON AND OF THE HOLY SPIRIT" (V. 19).

T he Protestant Reformers accepted the great ecumenical creeds, such as the Nicene Creed, that were formulated by the universal church early in church history. In these creeds, we find an emphasis on divine diversity—the Father, Son, and Holy Spirit are distinct persons. Yet these creeds also emphasize divine unity—the Father, Son, and Holy Spirit are one God. We may combine these ideas and say that the Father,

Son, and Holy Spirit are one God but that the Father is not the Son or the Holy Spirit, the Son is not the Father or the Holy Spirit, and the Holy Spirit is not the Father or the Son. We cannot fully understand how God can be both one in essence and three in person, but we will fail to affirm biblical monotheism if we deny either point.

Having looked at divine diversity yesterday, we will comment more on divine unity today as we look to Matthew 28:18–20. Here we have a key text that points to the unity of the three persons in light of Their distinctions. Notice that baptism is to be done in the name (singular) of the three (plural). The three persons share one name, and this name is none other than *Yahweh*, the covenant Lord of Israel. The name *Yahweh* in itself often refers to the divine essence, or the divine attributes, for it is by this name that God revealed His deity to Moses. "I AM WHO I AM" in Exodus 3:14 comes from the same Hebrew root for the name *Yahweh*, and it is a revelation of God's self-existence. *Yahweh* means that God has the power of being in Himself, that He depends on nothing other than Himself for His existence. We, on the other hand, depend on our parents and, ultimately, on God for our existence, and we need others to survive.

Divine unity, however, means that self-existence is not one particular component of God's being. Our doctrine of divine simplicity tells us that God's attributes are not separate parts of His being. His self-existence is His holiness is His justice is His goodness. All three persons share the one name *Yahweh* and thus the unity of the divine essence, and all three persons share the divine attributes equally. From all eternity, the Father's authority is the Son's authority is the Holy Spirit's authority. The Father's holiness is the Son's holiness is the Holy Spirit's holiness. Everything that God is essentially, the three persons are equally. None is more God or less God than any of the others.

FOR FURTHER STUDY

Isaiah 6:8; Luke 3:21-22; John 10:30; Galatians 3:20

APPLICATION

Jesus sometimes says that the Father is greater than He is (John 14:28). But that is not a reference to His divine essence; rather, in taking on our flesh, God the Son submits to the Father as a man, for that is what human beings are to do. Submission does

DAY 7 & 8

not refer to realities with respect to the divine essence, however. Thus, we worship the Son as fully God and do not think of Him as in any way less than the Father with respect to His essence.

DAY 9

MUTUAL INDWELLING

JOHN 14:8-11 "BELIEVE ME THAT I AM IN THE FATHER AND THE FATHER IS IN ME, OR ELSE BELIEVE ON ACCOUNT OF THE WORKS THEMSELVES" (V. 11).

T oday we will further consider how the oneness and the threeness of God are related. It is easy to focus on the unity of the Godhead at the expense of the distinctions between the persons and so miss the individual persons and Their relations to one another. The result can be a practical modalism that sees God as just like a man who merely holds three different roles depending on the context he is in and to whom he is relating. However true it may be that a man may be a father to his children, a son to his parents, and a husband to his wife all at the same time, that is not what we mean when we say that God is simultaneously Father, Son, and Holy Spirit.

Furthermore, we can also find it easy to emphasize the personal distinctions in a way that destroys Their unity. The result here is a practical tritheism that views God as a collection of individual, separable persons united by a common purpose. It is true that a football team is one team even though it is made up of several individual players, but the Trinity is not several individual, separable persons who each contribute Their own talents to the common mission of God.

Though we cannot fully conceive of how God can be one and three at the same time but not in the same sense, the concept of *perichōrēsis* helps us avoid Trinitarian errors. *Perichōrēsis* is a Greek term that refers to the mutual indwelling of the three persons of the Godhead. *Perichōrēsis* means that the Father is in the Son is in the Holy Spirit. We can distinguish the divine persons, but we cannot pull Them apart. They exist in one another, the Father dwelling completely in the Son and the Holy Spirit, the Son dwelling completely in the Father and the Holy Spirit, and the Holy Spirit dwelling completely in the Father and the Son. We find this concept of *perichōrēsis* in texts such as John 14:8–11, wherein the Son confesses that He is in the Father and the Father is in Him.

If there is only one divine essence and each of the three persons possesses it fully, *perichōrēsis* must be true. If each of the persons is all that God is in His essence and there is only one divine essence, the persons must be coextensive with one another. Without the mutual indwelling, They could be pulled apart, and if you pull Them apart, you do not have an undivided, singular divine essence.

FOR FURTHER STUDY

John 10:37-38; 14:18-20; 17:20-23; 2 Corinthians 5:19; Hebrews 1:3

APPLICATION

Our doctrine of *perichōrēsis* shows the perfect unity of God. Because the three persons cannot be pulled apart, we know that They are never at odds with one another. The Father is never opposed to the Son or the Holy Spirit. This perfect unity means that we can trust that when one of Them speaks, He is revealing the same purpose as the other two. God is not divided against Himself but speaks coherently and in an absolutely trustworthy manner.

DAY 10

DIVINE BEGOTTENNESS AND PROCESSION

JOHN 14:26 "THE HELPER, THE HOLY SPIRIT, WHOM THE FATHER WILL SEND IN MY NAME, HE WILL TEACH YOU ALL THINGS AND BRING TO YOUR REMEMBRANCE ALL THAT I HAVE SAID TO YOU."

All people possess a human nature, which includes attributes such as a mind, a body, and a will. So every human being is fully human regardless of gender, race, age, or other qualities. But even though every human being possesses a human nature, we have distinct attributes. For instance, the

DAY 9 & 10

mind of one human being is not the same as the mind of another. The same applies for every essential human attribute. We are all fully human, but there are differences between us in terms of our human attributes. We do not share the same mind, soul, body, will, or any other human attribute.

The unity of the divine persons with respect to the divine nature is wholly different. The three persons of the Trinity are all divine in that to have a divine nature is to be divine, yet the divine attributes are also identical between the three persons of the Godhead. The Father, Son, and Holy Spirit do not have three different minds; They have one identical mind. The same applies for every other divine attribute.

What makes the three persons of the Trinity differ from one another is a difference in relations, not in attributes. From the early church fathers through the Protestant Reformers to today, orthodox Christianity has said that what makes the Father the Father is that He is eternally unbegotten and what makes the Son the Son is that He is eternally begotten. Evidence for this is found in passages such as John 1:18, which in the KJV refers to the Son as "begotten." This is a better translation of the Greek than in some newer English versions, for the underlying Greek word has to do with generation. The Son is eternally generated by the Father. This generation, or begottenness, never had a beginning. The Son has always existed and has always been fully God even though He is begotten of the Father. And the Father has always begotten the Son such that the Son and the Father are both fully God.

Unbegottenness is the unique personal property of the Father, begottenness is the unique personal property of the Son, and procession is the unique personal property of the Holy Spirit. Following such texts as John 14:26, we say that the Holy Spirit proceeds from the Father and the Son. This passage, Dr. R.C. Sproul explains in his commentary *John*, says that "the Spirit is sent by both Father and Son," and Christian thinkers have seen this sending as reflective of a relationship of the Holy Spirit to Father and Son before time began. The Father and the Son sent the Holy Spirit at Pentecost because He has proceeded from Them from all eternity.

FOR
FURTHER
STUDY

John 3:16;
Acts 13:33

Why should we care to know these things about divine unity and distinction? It is not merely to fill our heads with theological knowledge. These concepts give us a further glimpse at who God is, allowing us to be filled with awe at how much greater God is than we can imagine. Knowing His set-apartness moves us to worship Him for His greatness, and thus we fulfill the purpose for which we were made.

DAY 11

THE TRINITY AND CREATION

GENESIS 1:1-2 "IN THE BEGINNING, GOD CREATED THE
HEAVENS AND THE EARTH. THE EARTH WAS WITHOUT FORM
AND VOID, AND DARKNESS WAS OVER THE FACE OF THE
DEEP. AND THE SPIRIT OF GOD WAS HOVERING OVER THE
FACE OF THE WATERS."

D uring His earthly life and ministry, Jesus said, "This is eternal life, that they know you, the only true God, and Jesus Christ whom you have sent" (John 17:3). To know God truly is to know His salvation, so when we are dealing with the doctrine of the Trinity, we are dealing with matters essential to our being redeemed.

Because of the distinction between the Creator and His creation, we can know God only as He reveals Himself. With Scripture, both the early church fathers and the Protestant Reformers teach us that God reveals Himself through His work in the world, particularly through His acts of creation and redemption. The way in which the Bible describes these activities helps us to have a better understanding of our Maker both in His oneness and in His threeness.

Today we will look at the revelation of our triune God in His work of creation. Note that Scripture attributes creation to each of the three persons. In Genesis 1:1–2, for example, we read that the Spirit of God—the Holy Spirit—hovered over the primordial

I

DAY 10 & 11

waters at the moment of creation, pointing to His intimate involvement in the seven-day process of making the earth and filling it with life. John 1:1–3 refers to God the Father and the Son ("the Word") at the beginning of creation, indicating that the Father made all things through the Son and that nothing was created apart from the agency of the Son.

In many places, Scripture attributes the work of creation particularly to the Father (see Eph. 3:9, for instance). But the references to all three persons of the Holy Trinity and Their involvement in creation show us that while the work of creation may reveal the Father in particular, creation is something that all three persons do in common. This must be so, for if God is one, then each person of the Godhead must be involved in everything that God does. When the Father acts, the Son and the Holy Spirit act as well. Father, Son, and Spirit are identical in Their attributes, so if the Father exercises His omnipotence to create, the Son and the Spirit do so as well because the omnipotence of the Father is the omnipotence of the Son is the omnipotence of the Spirit. Traditionally, this coworking of the three persons of the Godhead is known as the doctrine of *inseparable operations*.

FOR
FURTHER
STUDY

Psalm
104:30;
Isaiah
45:7; Malachi 2:10;
Colossians
1:15-16

APPLICATION

Because the three persons of the Trinity work in common, God is never at odds with Himself. One person does not coerce the others, but all three work in tandem to achieve Their common purposes. As His bride, we who form His church should strive for such unity of purpose that we might reflect His perfect unity to the world around us.

DAY 12

THE TRINITY AND ATONEMENT

HEBREWS 9:13-14 "IF THE BLOOD OF GOATS AND BULLS, AND THE SPRINKLING OF DEFILED PERSONS WITH THE ASHES OF A HEIFER, SANCTIFY FOR THE PURIFICATION OF THE FLESH, HOW MUCH MORE WILL THE BLOOD OF CHRIST, WHO

THROUGH THE ETERNAL SPIRIT OFFERED HIMSELF WITH-
OUT BLEMISH TO GOD, PURIFY OUR CONSCIENCE FROM DEAD
WORKS TO SERVE THE LIVING GOD."

G od is one in His essence, and an important ramification of this is that whenever He acts in relation to things outside Himself (*ad extra*), each of the three persons acts insepa-rably with the others. This manner of working is not akin to the work of a committee, wherein different members each contrib-ute their different gifts and talents to a cooperative endeavor, for the oneness of God means that the attributes of the three persons are identical. Father, Son, and Holy Spirit all have the same will, wisdom, power, holiness, and so forth. Yet this manner of insepa-rable operations is also not a monochrome activity wherein you cannot distinguish the three persons of the Trinity. Each person exercises the same divine attributes, but each does so in a man-ner that is peculiar to His person.

This is difficult to conceptualize, but it is somewhat easier to conceive when we look at the work of atonement. Although it is the incarnate Son, touching His human nature, who atones for our sin, all three persons work inseparably to effect the atone-ment that secures our salvation. Both Father and Son offer up the Son for our redemption, the Father as the subject who offers and the Son as both the subject who offers and the object who, touch-ing His human nature, is offered (Rom. 8:31–32; Heb. 9:13–14). And when the Father and Son offer up the Son, They do so in the Spirit, who by His "efficacious power" makes Christ's death as a man under divine wrath saving for us (Calvin; see Heb. 9:13–14). Atonement is from the Father through the Son who is offered in the Spirit for our salvation. It is a work of holy love by all three persons of the Trinity.

Yet the inseparable work of the divine persons does not exclude uniqueness among Them. One early church heresy, Patripas-sianism, collapsed the particularity of each Trinitarian person's manner of acting in the inseparable operation of atonement by saying that both Father and Son suffered. This was wrong because the particularity of the Son's manner of acting and His unique

I

DAY 11 & 12

possession of a human nature means that only Christ suffered. But Christ did not suffer with respect to His deity. The divine nature cannot change, so it cannot be subjected to suffering. Christ suffered on the cross touching only His human nature, not His divine nature. Human nature is changeable, so it can be subjected to suffering, and the Father did not unite to His person a human nature but only the Son. So the Father did not suffer on the cross but only Christ, and then only touching His humanity.

APPLICATION

Touching His divine nature, it was impossible for Christ to die. Touching His human nature, Christ could and did die. Christ could atone for our sin because He was truly man, but He was offered up for our salvation by all three members of the Trinity. In the humanity of Christ, God bore His own curse against sin, and now we live because of His work. Let us praise our Creator for His salvation.

FOR FURTHER STUDY

Genesis 15; Isaiah 53; Mark 10:45; 1 Peter 2:24

DAY 13

THE TRINITY AND REDEMPTION

JUDE 5 "I WANT TO REMIND YOU, ALTHOUGH YOU ONCE FULLY KNEW IT, THAT JESUS, WHO SAVED A PEOPLE OUT OF THE LAND OF EGYPT, AFTERWARD DESTROYED THOSE WHO DID NOT BELIEVE."

A s a cornerstone of Trinitarian theology, the doctrine of inseparable operations is necessary for maintaining an accurate view of God in both His unity of essence and His diversity of person. This doctrine, which says that each person of the Trinity acts inseparably with the others in every act of God with respect to things outside Himself, helps us understand that each person is involved in everything God does in a manner that is appropriate to that person. Every action of God is from the Father through the Son and in the Holy Spirit, and this is an order that is inherent to God's triune identity. Each person exercises the same divine attributes, but each does so in a manner fitting to His unique personal properties.

We have seen the doctrine of inseparable operations in both creation and atonement, and today we will look at the doctrine as it is revealed in the work of redemption more generally. Although atonement is essential to God's work of redemption, it is not identical to it. Redemption is a greater whole, of which atonement is one part. Redemption also involves things such as rescue from bondage, the resurrection of our bodies, and more (Ex. 20:2; Rom. 8:23).

Today's passage attributes the work of rescuing the Israelites from Egyptian slavery to Jesus (Jude 5), a particularly strong way of asserting His deity, since the Old Testament says that Yahweh, the covenant Lord of Israel, saved His people from Egypt (Deut. 5:6). Of course, we also know that the Lord went before His people as a pillar of fire when He led them out of Egypt (Ex. 13:21), pointing us to the activity of the Holy Spirit in light of the Spirit's association with supernatural fire (Luke 3:16; Acts 2:1–4). Given that Jesus often refers to the God of Israel as "Father," we thus see the involvement of all three persons in the work of redeeming the people of God from Egypt and, more generally, from sin and death.

The Scriptures often associate particular aspects of redemption, such as sanctification, with the Holy Spirit (2 Thess. 2:13). This is because the work of sanctification reveals the Spirit in particular. Given inseparable operations, however, the Father and Son are also involved in everything the Spirit does. From start to finish, redemption is the work of the triune God. It is from the Father, through the Son, and in the Holy Spirit that we are redeemed.

FOR FURTHER STUDY

Psalm 51:7;
Ezekiel 37:23;
Romans 14:17;
1 Timothy 4:1-5

APPLICATION

God's people are important to Him. That is proved in the fact that all three persons act to save us. We are not important to the Lord because of anything we are in ourselves. Rather, having decided to save us, God makes us important to Him. Because all of God is involved in our salvation, we know that He pays attention to whatever we are doing, saying, or thinking.

DAY 12 & 13

THE TRINITY AND CHRISTIAN UNITY

EPHESIANS 2:18 "THROUGH [CHRIST] WE BOTH HAVE ACCESS
IN ONE SPIRIT TO THE FATHER."

F ather, Son, and Holy Spirit worked inseparably in creation, making the universe out of nothing. The three persons also worked inseparably in bringing about atonement for our sin, offering up Christ to satisfy divine justice in the face of our sin. They work inseparably in all aspects of redemption, in fact, including our sanctification.

In Ephesians 2:18, the Apostle Paul tells us that the three persons also work as one in bringing unity between Christians. The context of this text is God's purpose to dissolve the wall between Jews and gentiles and to make them one people of God in Christ (vv. 11–22). Today's passage emphasizes the theological grounding of our unity in Christ. Whether we are Jew or gentile, we have access to God the Father in the same way—namely, in one Spirit through Christ. Christian unity is a consequence of our salvation, which comes from the Father through Christ in the ministry of the Holy Spirit. We enjoy this salvation by means of our regeneration in and by the Spirit, who brings us to Christ, through whom we are reconciled to the Father and brought back into a right relationship with God. The means of the triune God's working is from the Father through the Son and in the Spirit. The means by which salvation is applied to us and made effective operates in reverse. It is in the power of the Spirit, who brings us through Christ to the Father.

Because all Christians are brought to eternal life in the same way, there can ultimately be no divisions between Christians. We are being built into one body in Christ (v. 16). This does not mean a monolithic unity. As with the operation of the Trinity, there is diversity. But this diversity will not finally compromise our unity as Christians are more and more knit together as one people. We will be one in belief, one in worship, and one in love for our Creator.

It must be admitted that we do not now see much Christian unity. The visible church is divided. Invisibly, we are already one. All true believers in Christ are united to Him and, as a consequence, are united to one another as well. But the presence of sin and error keeps us from realizing this invisible unity in all its visible fullness. But our triune God has already torn down the divisions between believers, and even now He is laboring to make us one in His truth. This is a process that will not be finished until Christ returns, but rest assured, it will finally be accomplished.

FOR FURTHER STUDY

Ezekiel 37:15-28; 1 Corinthians 12:12-31; Ephesians 4:1-16

APPLICATION

God is truth, so the unity that He is effecting between believers is a unity grounded in truth. Father, Son, and Holy Spirit do not unite people by neglecting truth, so where we see essential truths being ignored or downplayed, we know that whatever "unity" is produced is not truly the work of God. Let us strive for unity with other believers, but always in a way that honors the love of truth shared by the three persons of our triune Creator.

DAY 15

THE TRINITY AND GOD'S LOVE FOR HIS PEOPLE

JOHN 17:20-26 "THE GLORY THAT YOU HAVE GIVEN ME I HAVE GIVEN TO THEM, THAT THEY MAY BE ONE EVEN AS WE ARE ONE, I IN THEM AND YOU IN ME, THAT THEY MAY BECOME PERFECTLY ONE, SO THAT THE WORLD MAY KNOW THAT YOU SENT ME AND LOVED THEM EVEN AS YOU LOVED ME" (VV. 22-23).

The doctrine of the Trinity is not an exercise in theological abstraction. Rather, it is vital for understanding God's character, purposes, and relationship with His people. One of the key insights of Trinitarian theology is that what Christ enjoys by nature, we enjoy by grace. As we look at today's passage, we see the Son referencing the love that the Father had

DAY 14 & 15

for Him from all eternity, love for the Son that preceded the Father's sending Him into the world (John 17:23). Because of the personal relations between the three persons of the Trinity, we must understand that this love of the Father for the Son is eternal, without beginning or end. To be the eternally unbegotten Father is to love the Son, and to be the eternally begotten Son is to love the Father.

God's love for us, however, is of a different order. It is love born of grace. Father, Son, and Holy Spirit would still be Father, Son, and Holy Spirit even if God had never chosen to love us. Yet one of the most wondrous aspects of our salvation is that when God chooses to love His people, it is with love that is the same in character as the intra-Trinitarian love between Father, Son, and Holy Spirit. Another way of putting this is to say that the relationship that the Son enjoys with the Father by virtue of His being the eternal Son, we enjoy by grace. In other words, the Father by grace—and by grace alone—showers on us the same love that He has for the Son. Speaking of us, Jesus said to the Father, "You … loved them even as you loved me" (v. 23).

John Calvin reminds us that we enjoy this love not because we are inherently lovable but because we are united to Christ. Because we are in Christ by faith, we are God's beloved children (John 1:12–13). God loves us with an enduring, undefeatable love because of Jesus. Calvin writes, "That love which the heavenly Father bears towards the Head is extended to all the members, so that he loves none but in Christ."

FOR FURTHER STUDY

Jeremiah 31:3b; 1 John 3:1a

APPLICATION

That the Father loves us—by grace—with the love He has for the Son is some of the best news we could ever hear. The Father cannot stop loving the Son, so if He chooses to set such love on us, He cannot stop loving us either. We persevere and have assurance because God loves us with an everlasting love. Let us be grateful for this love and call others to trust in Christ that they would know this love as well.

OUR INCOMPREHENSIBLE GOD

PSALM 145:3 "GREAT IS THE Lord, AND GREATLY TO BE
PRAISED, AND HIS GREATNESS IS UNSEARCHABLE."

o get a better grasp of the historic Christian view of God's
attributes and their biblical foundation, we will now
spend a few days looking at our Lord's character with the
help of *The Attributes of God*, a teaching series by Dr. R.C. Sproul.

At the outset, we cannot ignore that the study of God's attributes has fallen on hard times in the church and culture. This
is due in part to a shift from a focus on God in our worship to
man-centered approaches that make little of the glory of the Lord.
Moreover, religious skepticism that says that we cannot know
anything definitive about our Creator pervades Western culture.
The idea that God has revealed Himself through His prophets
and His Apostles is a ridiculous notion for many people. Even
harder to believe is that salvation is found only in Christ (John
14:6). People are happy to think of Jesus as offering one way of
salvation among many, but few are willing to see our Lord as
God's final revelation, believing that we are all finding our own
path to God, however we conceive of Him.

In sum, many people have relegated God to the realm of the
unknowable, and many professing Christians have followed suit.
God, after all, is incomprehensible, is He not? Yes, He is, but God's
being incomprehensible does not mean that He is unknowable.
Without a doubt, God is far beyond our understanding. Our finite
minds cannot fully grasp the depths of His being. Nevertheless,
we can know something about God. Since we are created in His
image (Gen. 1:26–27), we can know Him truly, if not fully.

We can know God, and Scripture calls us to pursue the knowledge of Him and His ways (Hos. 6:3; Matt. 11:27; John 12:45). Even
so, as the psalmist tells us, God's greatness is unsearchable (Ps.
145:3). When it comes to knowing God, there will always be more

I

DAY 15 & 16

GOD

for us to learn, even in eternity. We will plumb the depths of His
character, learning more and more that our Creator is infinitely
more glorious than we could ever imagine.

APPLICATION
God is unlike anything else that we can study. We can master
other subjects, but we can never master the Lord. His incomprehensibility means that there will always be new things for us to
learn about Him. Thus, we dare not think we have ever arrived
at the point where we know God fully. We must study His Word
deeply so that we would know Him better every day.

DAY 17

SPEAKING ABOUT GOD

PSALM 18 "I LOVE YOU, O LORD, MY STRENGTH. THE LORD IS
MY ROCK AND MY FORTRESS AND MY DELIVERER, MY GOD, MY
ROCK, IN WHOM I TAKE REFUGE, MY SHIELD, AND THE HORN
OF MY SALVATION, MY STRONGHOLD" (VV. 1-2).

Human beings use language to communicate, and this is
as true when they are doing theology as when they are
speaking about other topics. For centuries, people took
it for granted that human language was an adequate vehicle for
speaking about God, but in the twentieth century, things began
to change. Philosophers of religion and certain theologians began
to question whether human speech could convey truth about
our Creator. This led to a full-scale rejection of traditional ways
of talking about God and His attributes at seminaries that had
capitulated to theological modernism. Since human language was
thought to be incapable of saying anything definitive about the
Lord, thinkers began to view traditional theological categories
with great skepticism.

Moreover, theology became increasingly seen as a science in
which we do our best to say something about God as we imagine

FOR FURTHER STUDY
Job 26; 38-42; Isaiah 55:8-9; John 1:18; 1 Corinthians 2:11

Him, not as a discipline in which we do our best to understand God as He reveals Himself. Liberal theologians such as Paul Tillich eschewed the personal language about God found in Scripture in favor of impersonal designations such as God as the "ground of all being," and even then, these designations were virtually emptied of whatever biblical content might have remained.

As finite creatures, we use language that has limits when it comes to portraying God's attributes. But these limits do not make human speech worthless as an instrument of speaking truth about God. Since God made us in His image (Gen. 1:26–27), He has made us able to communicate in true and meaningful ways when we talk about Him.

Traditionally, theologians have said that human language about God is analogical language. To speak analogically is to use the same word to describe two different things, and yet the word is not used in exactly the same way for each thing under discussion. For example, we can speak of "good students" and "good dogs," meaning that both students and dogs can be obedient. Yet the obedience of students and the obedience of dogs, though similar, are of different orders. Both may obey commands, but we look for students to (eventually) obey as the result of sound moral reasoning and not merely out of a basic system of rewards and punishment.

When David refers to God as a "rock" in Psalm 18:2, he is speaking analogically. He is saying that like a rock, the Lord is firm and unshakable. God is like a rock in that way, but He is not literally a stone or a formation of minerals.

FOR FURTHER STUDY

Psalm 27:1; Isaiah 64:8; John 10:1-21; 1 Corinthians 10:4b

APPLICATION

Analogical speech about God has its limits, but it is fully adequate to tell us truth about the Lord. As we hear God referred to as a rock, a light, a shepherd, and a host of other metaphors, we should think carefully on how the Lord is like such things. That will enrich our view of God and our prayers and worship.

I

DAY 16 & 17

THE GOD WHO NEVER CHANGES

MALACHI 3:6 "I THE LORD DO NOT CHANGE; THEREFORE YOU, O CHILDREN OF JACOB, ARE NOT CONSUMED."

T he only thing constant is change." This saying is attributed to the Greek philosopher Heraclitus, one of the most significant Western thinkers to have lived before Socrates, Plato, and Aristotle. In making such a statement, Heraclitus captured what many others have also recognized—namely, that there is precious little that is stable in the world around us. Even the mountains, which appear to be so unchanging, are over millennia subject to erosion and other effects that slowly but surely alter their shape. But it is not just the world outside us that is unstable. Over time, we ourselves also experience physical, mental, moral, and spiritual changes.

Such realities drive us to seek stability. Because of sin, however, we tend to look for permanence in things that are also changing. Whether it is a relationship, our bank balances, familiar surroundings, or something else, we all too readily seek stability in the created realm. And moreover, we are eventually disappointed by such things, for everything in creation is subject to change.

To find true stability and permanence, we must look beyond the created order to its Creator, for as Scripture tells us, God is unchanging. As we read in Malachi 3:6, the Lord God Almighty does not change. And as the prophet tells us, that should be a great comfort to God's people. Jacob was not consumed because of the Lord's unchanging nature. The old covenant community deserved destruction because of its great sin, but God did not utterly destroy them. He had made a covenant with them, and because He is unchanging He could not break His promises to preserve them (see Gen. 15). As Christians, we serve the same unchanging God who kept His promises to Israel.

Summarizing the witness of Scripture, question and answer 4 of the Westminster Shorter Catechism states that God is "unchangeable in his being, wisdom, power, holiness, justice, goodness and truth." Our Lord is immutable—His character and being can experience no change or mutation (see Heb. 1:10–12). God cannot grow more or less powerful. He can never cease to be holy, just, good, or true. His wisdom and knowledge cannot be increased or decreased.

God's unchangeability is bad news for impenitent people, for it means that the Lord will not overlook their sin. But our Lord's immutability is good news for those who trust Him. It means that He cannot fail to keep His promises to forgive us and to protect us forever (Ps. 46; Isa. 55:6–7).

FOR FURTHER STUDY

Lamentations 3:22-23; Acts 4:11; Hebrews 13:8

APPLICATION
We live in a fallen world, and so it is easy to be fearful. Change is ever present, and not every change is positive. If we trust in Christ, however, we have no reason to be afraid. We are relying on the One who is incapable of changing and who will never allow His promises to fail. When we are fearful, let us remember that God and His goodness to us are unchanging; thus, we are ever secure in Him.

DAY 19

TRUTH HIMSELF

JOHN 14:6-7 "JESUS SAID TO [THOMAS], 'I AM THE WAY, AND THE TRUTH, AND THE LIFE. NO ONE COMES TO THE FATHER EXCEPT THROUGH ME. IF YOU HAD KNOWN ME, YOU WOULD HAVE KNOWN MY FATHER ALSO. FROM NOW ON YOU DO KNOW HIM AND HAVE SEEN HIM.'"

S acred Scripture emphasizes many themes, and one of the truths we find highlighted repeatedly throughout the Bible is the sanctity of truth. Given what John 14:6–7 tells us, this emphasis on truth makes perfect sense. After all, Jesus refers to Himself as "the truth," and since Jesus is God incarnate, we see that truth is ultimately a person. Our personal Creator is truth Himself.

I

DAY 18 & 19

Truth is fundamental to who God is as God. We see that the Word of God teaches us this in many ways. The Lord's chief enemy—Satan—is a "liar and the father of lies" (8:44). Since God is utterly opposed to all that Satan is and stands for, He must be nothing other than the truth. Because God is truth, His Word is truth (Ps. 119:160). The Lord comes near to bless only those who invoke His name in truth (145:18). In fact, truth is so important to God that He is willing to swear an oath to prove His own truthfulness. The Lord swore by Himself—for there is none higher by whom He may swear—to assure Abraham that He would keep His promises to the patriarch (Heb. 6:13–18; see Gen. 15).

Because truth is ultimately a person—God is truth—we find that truth consists of both propositions that are spoken or written and actions that people perform. God's written Word—Scripture—is truth, and it comes to us in propositional form. It is inspired such that it is without error and completely sufficient to equip us for every good work (2 Tim. 3:16–17). But we have not really known the truth of God's Word if we do not seek to put it into practice. We must love in deed and in truth, and since love encompasses actions, so also does truth. We are to walk in the Lord's true way, and this means a life of repentance in which we seek to do what God commands and repent when we fail to do so (Ps. 86:11; 1 John 1:5–10).

God Himself is truth, so there is no standard outside the Lord to which we may appeal for objective truth. Our Lord, as the Creator, defines reality, so truth can never be opposed to what He has revealed. When our conclusions do not seem to match His revelation, then we have drawn the wrong conclusions or we have failed to understand the teaching of His revelation properly. But our failures to comprehend His truth are our failures; they do not call His revealed truth into question. Let us study Scripture, confident in its truth, knowing that the Holy Spirit will help us to know His truth (1 Cor. 2:6–16).

FOR FURTHER STUDY

Isaiah 45:19; Jeremiah 5:3; John 16:13; 2 John 4-11

APPLICATION

Not only must we study the truth, but we must also love the truth. If we refuse to love the truth (2 Thess. 2:10), we will not be saved. As we seek to know God's truth, let us pray that the Lord would give us a love for His truth—even His hard truths—that we would serve Him faithfully and shine the light of His wisdom in this dark world.

DIVINE INFINITY

PSALM 147:5 "GREAT IS OUR LORD, AND ABUNDANT IN POWER; HIS UNDERSTANDING IS BEYOND MEASURE."

P rofessional theologians often distinguish between theology that proceeds by way of affirmation and theology that proceeds by way of negation. Theology done by affirmation seeks to say what God is. Such theology is also known as *cataphatic theology* and might include statements such as "God is good" and "God is holy."

Theology that proceeds by way of negation endeavors to say what God is not. Also known as *apophatic theology*, this theology of negation appears in statements such as "God is immutable," which means that God is without change or without mutation. Another apophatic statement would be "God is immaterial"—that is, God is not a material being or made of physical matter.

Today we are considering an apophatic statement with respect to God's attributes: God is infinite. Simply put, to say that God is infinite is to say that He is not a finite being. The Lord has no limitations; as Psalm 147:5 puts it, the Lord "is beyond measure." Something or someone that is beyond all human measure is infinite by definition. No matter how hard we try to "measure" God, He will always go beyond us.

Divine infinity is among the most difficult of God's attributes for us to conceptualize. It is nearly impossible for us to conceive of a being who has no limitations. We have limited life spans and must make choices on how to allocate limited resources. The distance between Orlando and Moscow might be vast, but

I

DAY 19 & 20

it can still be measured. Once we reach the limit of the measurement, we will arrive in the city to which we are traveling. Even the largest homes are limited in space, having walls that define the boundaries of the structure. But the Lord transcends every finite category we can think of. He cannot be contained in space, in our minds, or in any other place.

God's infinity is a consequence of His greatness, and it is related to other attributes such as His being omnipotent, or all-powerful. If the personal Creator cannot be contained or measured, then He can exert power over all else. Nothing can trap Him, but He can set limits on His creation. God's infinity also drives us to humility. As we have seen, we can know God truly but not fully. If the Lord cannot be measured, there are always limits to our understanding of Him. This should make us humble, as we recognize that God stands over us and all creation, even going far beyond all that we can conceive.

FOR
FURTHER
STUDY
———
Psalm 93;
Romans
11:33

APPLICATION

God's being has no spatial limitations, but this does not mean that there are not some things that the Lord cannot do. Our Creator, for example, is incapable of doing evil. He is morally constrained by His own character, which is perfectly good and holy. Because this holy God is infinite, He can bring His holiness to bear anywhere. No act of goodness or evil escapes His notice, so we should strive to obey our infinite God so that we will please Him.

DAY 21

DIVINE OMNIPRESENCE

JEREMIAH 23:23-24 "AM I A GOD AT HAND, DECLARES THE LORD, AND NOT A GOD FAR AWAY? CAN A MAN HIDE HIMSELF IN SECRET PLACES SO THAT I CANNOT SEE HIM? DECLARES THE LORD. DO I NOT FILL HEAVEN AND EARTH? DECLARES THE LORD."

A s a being who is beyond measure, God cannot be contained in any finite space (Ps. 147:5). The fact that our Lord has no spatial limitations has certain consequences for how we understand His other attributes, with omnipresence being a logical counterpart to His infinity. If God cannot be confined in any finite space, it makes sense that He would be omnipresent—that is, present everywhere in creation. Today's passage is one of many texts in Scripture that reveal to us our Creator's omnipresence. There is no place that we can hide in all creation because God fills all creation. No matter where we go, there our God will be. He is not limited to only one place, so we cannot erect a barrier between ourselves and His presence. He transcends spatial limitations, and He is able to be in many places—indeed, everywhere—all at once.

Like divine infinity, however, divine omnipresence is a difficult concept to grasp. It would be a mistake, for example, to conceive of omnipresence as God's being like a gas that is diffused throughout the entire universe. In the first place, gases have material form even if they are often invisible to us, and God is immaterial. He is spirit (John 4:24). Moreover, when a gas is diffused throughout a particular area, no one space contains every gas molecule. When we think about oxygen in a room, the full quantity of oxygen is not gathered at one point in the corner. Instead, there are gas molecules throughout the room.

Omnipresence is altogether different because it means that the fullness of God is present everywhere. Everything that God is is fully present at each point in a given room, at every point in the building outside the room, and at every point outside the building. "More" of God is not found at point A than at point B. God and His attributes, including His holiness, wisdom, goodness, justice, knowledge, power, and so on, are fully present in His creation at every point. We often forget that the Lord is right at hand wherever we are, but our forgetfulness does not indicate His absence.

Of course, God reserves the right to make us feel His presence more strongly at certain times and in particular places than at others (see, for example, Ex. 3:1–4:17). But even if God "feels"

I

DAY 20 & 21

FOR
FURTHER
STUDY

Proverbs
15:3; Isa-
iah 57:15;
Matthew
18:20;
2 Cor-
inthians
6:14-7:1

more present here than He does over there, He is equally present in both places. Thus, He guides us wherever we go (Ps. 23).

APPLICATION

God's omnipresence is a comforting truth. If God is everywhere,
then we know that He is never far away and can come quickly
to our aid. Because He is present everywhere, we can know that
He is acting in each and every place according to His holy will
for our good and to achieve His purposes. This is true even when
He seems to be far away.

DAY 22

THE GOODNESS OF GOD

JAMES 1:12-18 "EVERY GOOD GIFT AND EVERY PERFECT
GIFT IS FROM ABOVE, COMING DOWN FROM THE FATHER OF
LIGHTS, WITH WHOM THERE IS NO VARIATION OR SHADOW
DUE TO CHANGE" (V. 17).

Today we will be considering divine goodness. Our
Lord's goodness is one of the most frequently mentioned divine attributes in Scripture, but it is also one
that is all too often misunderstood. Therefore, it is vital for us
to remember that divine goodness, like God's other attributes,
cannot be considered in isolation. God will never exercise His
goodness in any way that would cause Him to set aside another
of His attributes.

As a divine attribute, goodness is first a description of God's
essential character. It means that the Lord is not evil, that He does
not love sin and, indeed, cannot even be tempted with evil (James
1:13). In this way, it is synonymous with some aspects of what
we typically call *divine holiness*, which refers both to God's being
set apart from everything else and to His moral character. Divine
goodness is also closely connected to divine justice. Goodness

abhors evil, so punishing evil is intrinsic to what it means for God to be good and just (Ex. 34:6–7). The Lord forbids human judges from perverting justice (23:2, 6), and that is not surprising because all His ways are just (Deut. 32:4). Consequently, divine wrath in the service of divine justice is one way in which God manifests His goodness to His creation.

Our Creator shows goodness in other ways as well. First, the Lord reveals His goodness in His benevolence to His creation. God's benevolence is the kindness that the Lord bestows on all people, and includes such things as His giving rain to both the just and the unjust (Matt. 5:45b). God has a specific love only for believers, and by this love He works out all things for the good of His people (John 1:12–13; Rom. 8:28). His benevolence, however, is a more generalized display of goodness that is not the love that leads to salvation.

God's special love for His people also manifests His goodness. This love is a holy love, which means that our sins are punished, but they are punished in Christ, who is the propitiation for our sins (Rom. 3:21–26). In saving us, God does not set aside His love for what is good and His hatred for what is evil, but He judges us in Christ so as to save us without compromising His justice. In His holy love, God also disciplines us for our good and His glory (Heb. 12:5–11).

Finally, God's mercy flows from His goodness. The Lord would still be good even if He never showed mercy, for mercy is not obligated (Rom. 9:14–24). Yet in His mercy to us, we see that He has purposed to be good in a special way to His people.

FOR FURTHER STUDY

Psalms 73:1; 86:5; Zechariah 9:16-17; Matthew 7:7-11; 1 Peter 2:1-3

APPLICATION

God's love is not a wishy-washy love that overlooks evil. Even in His love, God manifests His justice. He does not love sinners without dealing with their sin, and if we are in Christ, our sin has been dealt with in our Savior's atonement. Let us proclaim all aspects of God's goodness and call people to repent so that they will receive God's goodness and His mercy.

DAY 21 & 22

SALVATION

Scripture declares that "salvation belongs to the LORD" (Ps. 3:8; see Ps. 62:1; Rev. 7:10). When we study what the Bible has to say about salvation, we learn how the Creator of the universe is also the Redeemer of His chosen people.

Apart from God's intervention, fallen men and women are incapable of being in the right relationship to Him. Since the fall, all human beings are born in sin—that is, we are all born guilty of Adam's first sin and possess a fallen nature, and sin is compounded in our lives as we willfully violate God's law and seek our own desires (Rom. 5:12-21).

A holy, righteous God cannot ignore sin. Thus, humans are in a dire predicament, unable to save themselves and unable to achieve the righteousness that God requires. Yet in His grace, God has provided one—and only one—way for sinners to be reconciled to Him: through faith in the perfectly righteous life and substitutionary death of Jesus Christ to satisfy God's wrath and secure our righteousness (Rom. 1:16-3:31).

As we continue to examine the Christian life, we turn now to the glorious work that God accomplishes in the salvation of sinners, exploring its various facets so that we might rightly understand it and more heartily rejoice in God our Savior.

THE GRACE OF PREDESTINATION

EPHESIANS 1:3-4A "BLESSED BE THE GOD AND FATHER OF OUR LORD JESUS CHRIST, WHO HAS BLESSED US IN CHRIST WITH EVERY SPIRITUAL BLESSING IN THE HEAVENLY PLACES, EVEN AS HE CHOSE US IN HIM BEFORE THE FOUNDATION OF THE WORLD, THAT WE SHOULD BE HOLY AND BLAMELESS BEFORE HIM."

G race alone—the doctrine that we are saved only by God and not on account of anything we do—was a guiding principle of the Protestant Reformation. In opposition to medieval theologians who taught that God's grace was necessary but insufficient for salvation, the Reformers emphasized the Bible's stress on the necessity and sufficiency of grace for salvation. Many medieval theologians taught that we must contribute our own merit to achieve final salvation, but Reformation theologians stressed that even our grace-fueled obedience to God cannot be added to grace as a meritorious basis for eternal life. From first to last, salvation is the work only of God's grace.

Today's passage shows us that the Lord's saving grace begins operating for our salvation long before we are even born. Ephesians 1:3–4a tells us that even "before the foundation of the world," God chose those whom He would save from their sin and His wrath. In eternity past, the Lord numbered His people, choosing to set His saving love not on every human being but only on His elect.

Some people have taught that this election was based on God's foreseeing our obedience or on His knowing who would respond to the offer of salvation in Christ. Scripture denies these ideas forcefully. Paul tells us that we are chosen "in him"—namely, Christ (v. 4a). We were chosen not on account of what we have done but on account of what Christ has done. We were chosen not apart from Christ and His work for the salvation of His people but in Him as the recipients of the benefits of His work. And Paul also explains that we were chosen not because God knew we would be blameless and holy but in order that we would be blameless and holy. Our faith and growth in Christ are the result of our election to salvation, not the basis of it.

Lest we miss the point that we were chosen for redemption only by grace and not on account of anything we have done or because of our family history, Paul in Romans 9:6–13 uses Jacob and Esau as paradigms of God's electing grace. Jacob was chosen for salvation long before he could do anything good or bad. Esau, from the same family, was passed over for salvation before he could do anything good or bad. None of our actions, not even our good choice to believe in Jesus, moved the Lord to choose us for salvation.

FOR
FURTHER
STUDY

Isaiah
65:9; Mat-
thew 22:14;
Ephesians
1:11-12

APPLICATION

That nothing in us moved God to choose us for salvation is hard for many people to accept. But Scripture is clear that God chose us only on account of His good pleasure. We cannot take credit in any way for our salvation. We believe only because God first chose us. This should lead us to great humility and to never consider ourselves more highly than we ought.

`DAY 24`

GRACE AND REPROBATION

ROMANS 9:14-24 "WHAT IF GOD, DESIRING TO SHOW HIS WRATH AND TO MAKE KNOWN HIS POWER, HAS ENDURED WITH MUCH PATIENCE VESSELS OF WRATH PREPARED FOR DESTRUCTION, IN ORDER TO MAKE KNOWN THE RICHES OF HIS GLORY FOR VESSELS OF MERCY, WHICH HE HAS PREPARED BEFOREHAND FOR GLORY—EVEN US WHOM HE HAS CALLED, NOT FROM THE JEWS ONLY BUT ALSO FROM THE GENTILES?" (VV. 22-24).

II

S aving grace, God's unmerited favor toward those He has chosen to love unto salvation, cannot accurately be understood apart from our knowing what we deserve. So when the Apostle Paul explains the sheer graciousness of the Lord's grace and mercy, He sets it against the backdrop of what we have actually earned from His hand. Romans 9:14–24 is the key text here as the Apostle considers humanity as a whole in God's predestination of some people to redemption.

Paul emphasizes that those whom the Lord chooses to save and those whom He does not choose to save both come from the same lump of clay (vv. 21–24). What must be stressed here is that God, the potter, in choosing whom to save, has only one humanity to choose from and that this humanity is a fallen humanity. No ordinary human being has a right to eternal life, for all people (except Christ) are sinners in Adam (5:12–21). If God deals with one lump of humanity and this lump is not neutral (for it is impossible to be neutral with respect to God; see Matt. 12:30), then the lump is either righteous or fallen. If the lump were righteous, there would be no need for grace. No, the lump in view must be a fallen lump, for only in that context is grace necessary.

Since we deserve only eternal death apart from God's intervention, we cannot complain if the Lord shows grace and mercy only to some of us. By definition, grace and mercy are undeserved, so if the Lord chooses not to give them to someone, He is not depriving that person of what he has earned. God chooses some for salvation and chooses to pass by—to not elect for eternal life—others, in order to reveal Himself as both Savior and Judge (Rom. 9:14–21). The grace shown in predestination unto salvation has a flip side in reprobation, God's leaving some in their sins and to the just consequences of those sins.

Because election to salvation is by grace, it is not based on anything in us. It is unconditional. That is, God's purpose in choosing Joe for salvation instead of James is not because Joe is more righteous or smarter or for any other reason besides His choice to love Joe for the sake of His glory. But in an important respect, reprobation is unconditional as well. True, the reprobate do deserve punishment, but God does not pass over James and choose Joe because James is more evil than Joe is. In fact, many who end up in heaven committed worse sins than many of those who go to hell. That is because God's election is based not on the degree of our sin or our personal righteousness. It is based only on His free choice to forgive those whom He chooses to forgive.

FOR
FURTHER
STUDY

Malachi
1:1-5;
Matthew
11:25-
27; John
10:22-30;
1 Peter
2:8b

The elect get what they do not deserve—salvation; the reprobate get what they deserve—condemnation. The doctrine of election should not lead us to pride or to consider ourselves as inherently holier than others. It should be a continual reminder to us that we are among the worst of sinners and that we are in Christ only because God chooses to love undeserving sinners. May the doctrine of election make us more aware of our sin and the grace of the Lord.

DAY 25

THE GRACE OF REGENERATION

EPHESIANS 2:1-9 "GOD, BEING RICH IN MERCY, BECAUSE OF THE GREAT LOVE WITH WHICH HE LOVED US, EVEN WHEN WE WERE DEAD IN OUR TRESPASSES, MADE US ALIVE TOGETHER WITH CHRIST—BY GRACE YOU HAVE BEEN SAVED" (VV. 4-5).

John Calvin, commenting on today's passage, makes the point that "everything connected with our salvation ought to be ascribed to God as its author." This statement is quite radical in light of common beliefs about salvation that we find in the Christian community. Most professing Christians are happy to attribute their salvation to divine grace. Few would say that they deserve heaven. Yet when questions are asked about the reasons why people choose faith in Christ, many believers are unwilling to say that God chooses some for salvation or authors their decision to believe. In the name of a particular view of free will that says we must, at every point, have the equal ability to choose between right and wrong, many Christians end up denying—perhaps without meaning to—God's sovereign, effectual grace.

Calvin takes from Scripture his view that every part of salvation is authored by God. This includes even our decision to believe. We believe only because the Lord makes us willing to

II

25

DAY 24 & 25

believe. Apart from grace, we are fully unwilling to believe. Our hearts are dead in sin, and dead hearts—just like dead bodies—cannot move of their own accord (Eph. 2:1–3). We must not stretch the metaphor too far; Paul is not saying that human beings are unable to make choices without God's grace. Unredeemed sinners, after all, make choices every day. What the Apostle means is that unless God's grace resurrects our dead hearts, we cannot make decisions that are pleasing to the Lord. "Those who are in the flesh cannot please God" (Rom. 8:8), and to be dead in trespasses and sin is to be in or controlled by the flesh.

If we are dead with respect to the things of God, unable to choose what the Lord finds pleasing—and He certainly approves of the choice to repent and believe in Christ alone for salvation—then our Creator must intervene drastically if we are to be redeemed. He changes our hearts without our asking Him to do so, making us willing to believe. This work is referred to in theological categories as God's work of regeneration, and it is described in Ephesians 2:4–7. Even while we were dead in our trespasses, the Lord brought us to new spiritual life, and as a consequence, we believed. Faith does not precede regeneration. It is not that we believe and then our hearts are changed; rather, we believe after God first changes our hearts. Regeneration precedes faith, which is a gift, part of what is "not [our] own doing" (vv. 8–10). Having been given new hearts, we cannot help but believe.

FOR
FURTHER
STUDY

John 3:1-
8; James
1:18

APPLICATION

God's saving grace is not weak but powerful and effectual to save. It can bring dead souls to life, and since the life that God gives is far more powerful than death, no one to whom saving grace is shown will fail to be regenerated. If God wants to save someone, that person will be saved. No resistance to divine grace can endure. We therefore pray for God to change hearts, knowing that salvation is His powerful work alone.

THE GRACE OF JUSTIFICATION

TITUS 3:4-7 "BEING JUSTIFIED BY HIS GRACE WE MIGHT
BECOME HEIRS ACCORDING TO THE HOPE OF ETERNAL LIFE"
(V. 7).

F rom first to last, God saves His people by grace alone. In divine election, He chooses men and women in Christ for redemption based on nothing in them but only on account of His gracious choice to set His love on them (Rom. 9:1–29; Eph. 1:3–6). Furthermore, in regeneration, God acts alone and wholly by His grace. He takes hearts dead in sin and makes them alive unto Him, giving them the gifts of faith and repentance (Eph. 2:1–9). Through the reading and especially the preaching of His Word, God by His Holy Spirit makes us born again of imperishable seed (1 Peter 1:22–25). His saving grace finally overcomes the resistance of all those whom He has chosen to redeem, and they are brought to new spiritual life that cannot be lost.

Today's passage explains that as the Lord applies the salvation purchased by Christ to His people, our justification—being declared righteous and forgiven of sin—is also a work of grace (Titus 3:7). It is impossible to overstate this point, for justification by grace alone through faith alone, apart from our works, is central to the gospel. This is the doctrine that the Protestant Reformers proclaimed against the medieval system of salvation, which said that grace is necessary for justification but that our final justification also requires our good works.

When we study texts such as Titus 3:4–7, it is easy to understand why the Reformers were so insistent on the gracious character of justification. As verse 5 tells us, God saved us "not because of works done by us in righteousness." Paul sets up in this verse the antithesis to justification by grace alone. If justification is by grace, it cannot involve any of our own deeds of obedience, no matter how pleasing to the Lord they may be. To look to the works done

II

DAY 25 & 26

43

FOR
FURTHER
STUDY

Isaiah
53:11;
Luke 18:9-
14; Romans
3:21-26;
Galatians
5:4

by us in righteousness as the root of justification and not the fruit of justification is to take grace off the table. Our righteousness before God is wholly a gift. The righteousness of Christ is a perfect righteousness (2 Cor. 5:21), so not even our best works can be added to it. To try to add any works to the righteousness of Christ is, in fact, to take away from the righteousness of Christ. It is to say that what our perfect Savior has done is not perfect after all.

Our new hearts are a gift. Our faith is a gift. And our righteous status before God is a gift as well. Only by grace do we stand before God unafraid.

APPLICATION

We will cover justification in more detail in the weeks ahead. For now, let us note how critical it is that we know that our good works do not and cannot justify us. The very honor of Christ is at stake in this. If we suggest that our works are necessary for justification, we are saying that what Christ gives us is insufficient, which denigrates His work. By upholding justification by grace alone, we are honoring the Lord Jesus Christ.

DAY 27

THE GRACE OF SANCTIFICATION

PHILIPPIANS 2:12-13 "THEREFORE, MY BELOVED, AS YOU HAVE ALWAYS OBEYED, SO NOW, NOT ONLY AS IN MY PRESENCE BUT MUCH MORE IN MY ABSENCE, WORK OUT YOUR OWN SALVATION WITH FEAR AND TREMBLING, FOR IT IS GOD WHO WORKS IN YOU, BOTH TO WILL AND TO WORK FOR HIS GOOD PLEASURE."

W ith respect to salvation, it is important to see that we oppose grace and merit, not grace and human activity. What do we mean by this? At no point in salvation does our merit enter into the equation. We do not and cannot merit or earn election, regeneration, faith, justification, sanctification, or glorification. There are points in salvation, however, where we do act, though not in a meritorious way. For example, we act in the exercise of faith. We do something because we put our trust in Christ. Though faith is God's gracious gift, God does not believe for us. We believe. But—and this is essential—our believing is not meritorious. The Lord does not take our faith as a payment for eternal life. Faith merely lays hold of Christ and His righteousness, and that is what merits eternal life.

Another place in salvation where grace and human activity are not opposed is in our sanctification, our growth in Christ and progress in holiness over our lifetimes. Just consider Philippians 2:12–13, where Paul tells us to "work out [our] own salvation with fear and trembling." Clearly, Paul has some human activity in mind. But Paul stresses God's initiative. We work because God works in us. The Lord's grace is operative in sanctification. He works in us to give us the will to obey Him, and He works in us to produce good works of obedience. These good works are the result of grace, but they are not meritorious of salvation. God looks upon and is pleased with our sanctification, but it is not because we keep His commandments that we receive eternal life. We receive eternal life because Christ kept God's commandments perfectly.

Grace and our own merit are opposed at every point in salvation. We can make no claim on God. But grace does not mean that we are passive in the outworking of the Lord's redemption. At key points—such as sanctification—we act, not to earn our place in heaven, but because Christ has earned our place in heaven and because He is working in us to prepare us for heaven. God initiates, sustains, and completes our holiness. We act in a non-meritorious way to grow in the grace and knowledge of the Lord Jesus Christ, and we produce good works because God's sanctifying grace alone guarantees them.

FOR FURTHER STUDY

Deuteronomy 28:9;
Romans 8:13;
2 Corinthians 7:1;
Hebrews 13:20-21

APPLICATION

Until we are glorified, the presence of sin remains in us, affecting all that we do. Thus, our obedience cannot merit salvation because none of our obedience is perfect. But God is pleased to accept good works done in Christ and by grace, using them to conform us ever more to the Lord. So we act and obey not to earn heaven but because heaven has been earned and secured for us by Jesus.

II

DAY 26 & 27

THE GRACE OF PERSEVERANCE AND GLORIFICATION

PHILIPPIANS 1:6 "I AM SURE OF THIS, THAT HE WHO BEGAN A GOOD WORK IN YOU WILL BRING IT TO COMPLETION AT THE DAY OF JESUS CHRIST."

D uring the Protestant Reformation, the debate was never over the necessity of grace. To this day, both Roman Catholics and Protestants agree that divine grace is necessary for salvation. Neither group advocates a Pelagian view that would say that grace is helpful but not strictly necessary to be saved.

There was no real debate regarding the necessity of grace during the Reformation, but there was disagreement on the sufficiency of grace. To put the disagreement most simply, Rome said then and continues to say now that grace enables but does not compel salvation. Not everyone who receives the grace of God ends up in heaven. That is because grace in itself cannot initiate, sustain, or complete salvation without free human assent and cooperation. And since human assent and cooperation are not guaranteed by grace, many receive grace but do not persevere in faith. This understanding puts the final decision with respect to salvation in our hands. Though Roman Catholicism would not state it so crassly, its official teaching makes the human will decisive in redemption.

Magisterial Protestantism and its heirs in the Reformed tradition, however, argued for the necessity and sufficiency of grace in salvation. Grace enables and compels. Everyone to whom saving grace is shown perseveres to the end and dies in faith. Human beings act at various points in salvation, particularly in sanctification, but their salvation is not sustained by their cooperation. Rather, they continue to believe because God's grace is effectual and guarantees perseverance. As today's passage tells us, when the Lord initiates salvation, He always finishes what He starts (Phil. 1:6). He sustains and completes the redemption of all to whom redemption is given.

God keeps in salvation all those whom He saves. Everyone who is justified is also glorified; there is no such thing as a person who experiences conversion and justification but then falls away finally and fully from grace (Rom. 8:29–30). Many people make a false profession of faith and fall away because they were never truly saved to begin with (1 John 2:19). True, believers may succumb to significant sin. As Dr. R.C. Sproul says in his book *Can I Lose My Salvation?*, "Each and every Christian is subject to the possibility of a serious fall." But he also notes that no true Christian will experience a total fall from grace. God's grace will not let His people fall away finally. He loves us enough to guarantee our final redemption.

APPLICATION

Knowing that God will keep us in grace inspires us to work out our salvation, obeying Him as evidence that He is indeed preserving us. And when we see someone apparently fall from grace, that is our cue to pray for that person. We do not know whether God may yet restore that person, and we know that the Lord works through our prayers to accomplish His will.

FOR FURTHER STUDY

Psalms 37:28; 97:10; 145:20; Mark 4:1-20; Hebrews 10:39

DAY 29

THE TRUTH SHALL MAKE YOU FREE

JOHN 8:31-38 "TRULY, TRULY, I SAY TO YOU, EVERYONE WHO PRACTICES SIN IS A SLAVE TO SIN" (V. 34).

So that we might get a better grasp of the human condition and divine grace, we will now spend a few days considering the issues of grace, human freedom, and sin with the help of *Willing to Believe*, a teaching series by Dr. R.C. Sproul.

Scripture, we have seen, describes us as dead in sin apart from the grace of God (Eph. 2:1–3), meaning that we are unable to do any spiritual good unless the Lord intervenes. This is not a popular teaching in our day, but those who would resist our deadness in sin have an argument with Jesus Himself. As is

II

DAY 28 & 29

evident in today's passage, Paul's view of our deadness in sin was not original to him. Jesus taught the same thing during His earthly ministry.

John 8:31–38 describes the umbrage that many first-century Jews took when Jesus told them that they were enslaved. Hearing that they were slaves, many of our Lord's contemporaries responded in astonishment, for they were children of Abraham who had never personally experienced slavery. They lived long after the days of Israel's slavery in Egypt and dwelled in their homeland without being bought and sold by slave masters. But the slavery that Christ spoke of was not physical bondage; rather, He was talking about slavery to sin: "Everyone who practices sin is a slave to sin" (v. 34). Many first-century Jews saw themselves as inherently better than gentiles. They took pride in their status as God's chosen people and believed that they were not sinners as the gentile heathen were (see Gal. 2:15–21, where Paul adopts this view for the sake of arguing against it). That understanding, however, had no basis in Scripture or the history of Israel. So Jesus and the Apostles preached the radical message that all people are sinners and enslaved to wickedness until God acts to free them (John 8:36; Rev. 1:5).

FOR FURTHER STUDY

Lamentations 1:1; Romans 6:15-23; Titus 3:3; 2 Peter 2:19

It may not be popular to believe that all people are enslaved, but God's Word tells us that everyone is a slave/servant either to sin or to Christ (see Rom. 1:1, for example). Sinners believe that they can be free without being a slave of Christ, but ironically, seeking freedom outside of Christ leads only to greater bondage to sin and death (Gal. 4:21–31).

APPLICATION

Sin is a harsh master, leading its slaves finally to death. Christ, however, is a kind Master who gives us an easy yoke. His servants will experience not eternal death but eternal life. If we think that we can find freedom and life outside of Christ, we are fooling ourselves, so let us cast aside our sin and look for life only in Jesus. He alone can satisfy us this day and every day.

SLAVES TO SIN

1 CORINTHIANS 15:22 "AS IN ADAM ALL DIE, SO ALSO IN CHRIST SHALL ALL BE MADE ALIVE."

C hurch historians have often observed that there is no such thing as a completely new heresy. Their point is that the errors the church faces today are simply repackaged versions of heresies the church dealt with hundreds of years ago. And one of the most frequently recurring heresies is the one most closely associated with Pelagius.

Pelagius was a British monk who lived circa AD 354–420. He was a man zealous for good works and who was very concerned about what he perceived as moral laxity in the church of his day. In his theology, Pelagius stressed human ability, believing that if God commands people to do something, they must have the ability to do it without His assistance. After all, he reasoned, it would be unjust to command people to do something that they were unable to do, and since the Lord is just, His commands necessarily imply human ability.

Thus, Pelagius reacted strongly against the teaching of Augustine of Hippo, particularly Augustine's prayer "Grant what You command and command what You desire." Because of his view of human ability, Pelagius could not abide Augustine's asking the Lord to give him the ability and willingness to obey God's law. To ask for such enabling would mean that we are unable to do what is good in the Lord's eyes without the Lord's assistance.

Augustine prayed his prayer because he had a far greater respect for the power of sin than Pelagius did. Pelagius failed to reckon with the fall and original sin. Adam's failure, Paul tells us, results in all his natural descendants' being born as sinners. We are guilty as soon as we are conceived, for we are born in Adam and the guilt of his sin is imputed to us—those whom he represented before God in Eden. With guilt, we receive a corrupted nature that is

II

DAY 29 & 30

49

incapable of pleasing God (Rom. 5:12–21). "In Adam all die" (1 Cor. 15:22), and dead men can do nothing unless God brings them to new life. This means that in light of our postfall condition, Pelagius was wrong to suggest that God's commands imply human ability to keep them. In Adam, we chose to surrender our ability to obey, but God did not stop being the Lawgiver. He justly commands sinners to do what they cannot do because they willingly surrendered their ability to please Him.

Augustine asserted that divine grace is absolutely necessary for salvation. Because we are born slaves to sin, God must act to free us, or we will be slaves to evil forever.

APPLICATION

FOR
FURTHER
STUDY

Gene-
sis 6:5;
Ephesians
2:8-10

Few would claim the mantle of Pelagius today, but it is a common belief that God's commands imply our ability to obey. Thus, many people overestimate the degree to which they have kept God's law. We must have a strong, biblical doctrine of sin, or we will view ourselves more highly than we ought. Are you convinced that you are a sinner and without hope save for the grace of the Lord?

DAY 31

THE LOSS AND RESTORATION OF LIBERTY

GENESIS 3:6-7 "WHEN THE WOMAN SAW THAT THE TREE WAS GOOD FOR FOOD, AND THAT IT WAS A DELIGHT TO THE EYES, AND THAT THE TREE WAS TO BE DESIRED TO MAKE ONE WISE, SHE TOOK OF ITS FRUIT AND ATE, AND SHE ALSO GAVE SOME TO HER HUSBAND WHO WAS WITH HER, AND HE ATE. THEN THE EYES OF BOTH WERE OPENED, AND THEY KNEW THAT THEY WERE NAKED. AND THEY SEWED FIG LEAVES TOGETHER AND MADE THEMSELVES LOINCLOTHS."

 ugustine of Hippo rose to the challenge of opposing Pelagius during the early fifth century when Pelagius denied the necessity of grace for salvation. Although Pelagius believed that Adam had sinned in Eden, he did not see that first sin as having any radical consequences for Adam's descendants. It did not affect our ability to obey the Lord. Grace might be helpful, but it was not a necessity, for God's issuing of commandments even after the fall means that we are able in ourselves to keep them. Our free will—the equal ability to choose between good and evil—remained intact.

The great North African church leader could not be silent when he learned of Pelagius' teaching, for he had a far better grasp of biblical teaching than Pelagius did. In responding to Pelagius, Augustine formulated one of the most extensive treatments of original sin—how Adam's sin affects his natural descendants—in church history. Augustine faulted Pelagius for failing to make a distinction between free will and liberty. Free will, Augustine said, is simply the ability to make choices among several options, and human beings retain it after Adam's fall into transgression. What we lack apart from grace, however, is liberty. According to Augustine, liberty is the ability to choose what is good and pleasing to the Lord. True freedom consists in doing what our Creator approves of. So, Augustine said, we may have free will after Adam, but we are not truly free apart from grace.

Following Scripture, Augustine described the fourfold state of humanity. Before the fall, we were able to sin or not to sin (*posse peccare, posse non peccare*). We could resist temptation and obey God's command not to eat the forbidden fruit (Gen. 2:15–17). But in the fall, we lost that ability. Now, we are not able not to sin (*non posse non peccare*). In other words, without transformation by divine grace, the thoughts of our hearts are only evil continually (6:5). We are dead in sin and trespasses until the Lord sovereignly intervenes to give us new spiritual life (Eph. 2:1–10). At that point, we regain the ability not to sin (*posse non peccare*), but that does not mean that we will be sinless. Until we are brought into God's presence, sin remains and we will succumb to temptation from time to time. We engage in the lifelong battle against sin that Paul describes in Romans 7.

In our glorification, however, we will enjoy the truest freedom

FOR
FURTHER
STUDY
———
Isaiah
2:1-5;
Jeremiah
4:1-4;
James 4:1-
10; 1 John
3:2-3

possible, for we will be unable to sin (*non posse peccare*). We will practice only righteousness and will shine with the brightness of the stars, for we will be fully conformed to Christ (Dan. 12:3; Phil. 3:21).

APPLICATION

When Adam and Eve sinned, they tried to hide from God (Gen. 3:6–7). Since then, all people apart from grace have continued hiding from the Lord, seeking to avoid His law and His judgment. This is a futile effort, and thankfully, God brings us out of shame and hiding by His grace. We show that His grace is working in us by continually bringing our sin into His light through confession and repentance, trusting His promise to forgive us in Christ.

DAY 32

GOD'S INITIATING GRACE

1 JOHN 4:19 "WE LOVE BECAUSE HE FIRST LOVED US."

L argely due to the efforts of Augustine of Hippo, the Western church condemned Pelagius and his heresy, Pelagianism, at the Second Council of Orange in AD 529. The same council also condemned a weaker form of the Pelagian heresy that has come to be known as semi-Pelagianism.

Traditionally, most scholars have said that semi-Pelagianism originated in the writings of the French monk John Cassian, who lived at roughly the same time as Augustine and Pelagius, during the late fourth and early fifth centuries AD. Essentially, semi-Pelagianism tries to steer a middle ground between Pelagius and Augustine. While rejecting the Augustinian view of unconditional election to salvation, semi-Pelagianism nevertheless affirms the necessity of grace for salvation. The problem is that semi-Pelagian thought denies the radical depravity into which sin has plunged the human race. In semi-Pelagianism, grace is necessary but human beings take the first step toward God. Without the assistance of grace, fallen men and women retain the ability to seek the Lord of their own accord. They need grace to be saved, but God's grace does not take the initiative in salvation. It is available to all if they will just seek it out. This is different from Augustinian and biblical theology, which says that grace is selective and that the initiative is always the Lord's. He makes the first move in salvation. No sinner can seek God of his own accord, and the only people who seek Him are those whom He first sovereignly and effectually draws by His saving grace (see John 6:44).

At root, the real disagreement between semi-Pelagianism and Augustinianism has to do with whether God's saving grace in regeneration is synergistic or monergistic. Semi-Pelagians say that divine grace is fundamentally synergistic—God and human beings work together to bring about regeneration. Men and women seek God and then God responds with His grace. Augustinians, including Reformed thinkers such as John Calvin, affirm that divine grace is monergistic in regeneration. The Lord is the only One who works to bring about the new birth, and His grace finally saves all those to whom it is given. His grace is not given to everyone but only to the elect and then not because of anything in the elect themselves. To put it another way, biblical, Augustinian thought is insistent that we love God only because He first loved us (1 John 4:19) and that God guarantees that His elect will love Him, overcoming their resistance to His love.

FOR FURTHER STUDY

Ezekiel 34:11-16; Hosea 2:14-23; Luke 19:10; Romans 5:1-5

APPLICATION

Augustinianism and semi-Pelagianism ultimately disagree regarding the power of God's love and beauty. Is God's love so effectual and is He so lovely that those to whom He reveals His salvation cannot finally reject Him, or are His love and beauty of a lesser character that cannot convince everyone whom He wants to save? By upholding Augustinian thought, we are powerfully declaring the glorious love and beauty of our Creator.

II

32 & 31 DAY

53

GOD'S INTERVENING GRACE

ROMANS 3:10-11 "NONE IS RIGHTEOUS, NO, NOT ONE; NO
ONE UNDERSTANDS; NO ONE SEEKS FOR GOD."

P elagianism and semi-Pelagianism were condemned at the
Second Council of Orange in AD 529, and today Roman
Catholicism continues to affirm this condemnation. There
is a problem, however, as was noted in the Reformation and ever
since. Although Rome officially denies that it embraces Pelagian
and semi-Pelagian theology, aspects of its theology suggest that its
denial of semi-Pelagianism is merely formal, that in practice Roman
Catholic theology lapses back into a kind of semi-Pelagianism.

The matter is complex because Roman Catholicism is a complex
system, particularly in its teaching on grace and human freedom;
thus, it can be difficult to sort out what Rome is actually saying.
For example, classic Reformed theology posits a rather simple
distinction with respect to God's grace. There is common grace,
which is God's nonsaving benevolence to all creation, and saving
grace, which is God's special, effectual saving grace given only
to the elect. Roman Catholic theology, however, speaks of many
more kinds of grace—sanctifying grace, habitual grace, operative
grace, sacramental grace, prevenient grace, and others—some of
which can appear irresistible depending on the theologian that
one is reading.

Perhaps the best way to consider Rome's ambiguity is to examine
some of its official documents. For instance, the seventh canon of
the sixth session of the Council of Trent condemns anyone who
says "that all works done before justification, in whatever manner
they may be done, are truly sins, or merit the hatred of God; that
the more earnestly one strives to dispose himself for grace, the
more grievously he sins." Since in Roman Catholicism justification comes by the grace received in baptism, this canon suggests
that human beings are able to do what is truly good even before
justifying grace is given. This would contradict today's passage,
which says that no one does what is truly pleasing to God until

He intervenes to save (Rom. 3:10–11). On the other hand, the first canon of the same session of Trent condemns anyone who believes that he can be justified by works done without grace.

Apologists for Rome have suggested ways to fit all these things together. Nevertheless, such statements, plus Rome's condemnation of the more strongly Augustinian theology of the seventeenth-century Jansenists, make it hard to see how Rome has not embraced at least a lesser form of semi-Pelagianism. In Roman Catholic theology, people are not as fallen as the Bible says we are.

APPLICATION

Either God is the source of all good or He is not. If we deny the necessity of grace to do what the Lord considers truly good, then we end up calling into question whether He is the ultimate source of every good thing. It then makes it easy for us to claim the credit for the good that we do. Understanding our fallenness, that we will not seek God without His effectual grace, enables us to worship Him more fervently as the source of every good and perfect gift.

FOR FURTHER STUDY

Zechariah 12; 1 Corinthians 15:10; 2 Corinthians 9:8; Ephesians 2:8-10

DAY 34

ALL OF GRACE

TITUS 2:11 "THE GRACE OF GOD HAS APPEARED, BRINGING SALVATION FOR ALL PEOPLE."

E very discussion of divine grace must address the issue of how free the human will actually is after the fall of Adam. As we have seen, thinkers who have emphasized the enslavement of the human will to sin—including men such as Augustine, Martin Luther, John Calvin, and Jonathan Edwards— have never denied that human beings are free to make choices. Both human experience and the teaching of Scripture show us that even unregenerate people make real choices every day. The issue, according to these thinkers, is that our freedom is always limited in some way by our desires. To be free is to do what we

II

DAY 33 & 34

most want to do; the problem is that apart from grace, the only thing we want to do is sin. To do what is truly good and pleasing to God, grace must change our hearts, and for these thinkers, divine grace always produces a change in the hearts of the elect such that they inevitably trust Christ and persevere in faith.

Despite its clear biblical foundations in passages such as Ephesians 2:1–10, the understanding that saving grace is ultimately irresistible—that it effectually overcomes all our resistance to it and brings us to salvation—remains a minority position among professing evangelical Christians. Today, most people who identify as evangelicals adopt the views of grace and freedom propounded by men such as Jacob Arminius and John Wesley.

Arminius and Wesley understood the necessity of grace for salvation, but they wanted to preserve our ability to accept or reject saving grace. Thus, based on passages such as Titus 2:11, they proposed what is called "prevenient grace," a grace given to all people that frees us enough from our bondage to sin that we have the ability to choose Christ but that does not finally persuade us to make that choice or guarantee that we will be saved. (Many Roman Catholics speak of God's prevenient grace in a similar way.) This view has the advantage of stating that no one can be saved without grace or even God's initiative in freeing our wills just enough to choose Him. The problem is that the doctrine of prevenient grace ends up creating a kind of de facto semi-Pelagianism. If prevenient grace is indiscriminate and merely restores our ability to choose, then it is hard to see how salvation is truly all of grace. In a sense, God takes the first step in redemption by bestowing prevenient grace, but the final reason why anyone is saved must be located in our will, in our willingness to move toward God that we somehow, with the help of grace, work up in ourselves.

FOR
FURTHER
STUDY

Genesis
12:1-9;
Isaiah
6:1-8; Acts
9:1-22;
22:1-21;
26:1-23

APPLICATION

Passages such as Titus 2:11 are invoked as proof of prevenient grace, but the biblical doctrine of election forces us to reject Arminian and Wesleyan interpretations. When Paul says that the grace of God has brought salvation to all people, he must mean that God has saved all kinds of people. Salvation is not restricted to one gender, ethnicity, or socioeconomic group, so we must preach the gospel to people of every background.

THE NECESSITY OF GRACE

ROMANS 12:3 "BY THE GRACE GIVEN TO ME I SAY TO EVERY-ONE AMONG YOU NOT TO THINK OF HIMSELF MORE HIGHLY THAN HE OUGHT TO THINK, BUT TO THINK WITH SOBER JUDGMENT, EACH ACCORDING TO THE MEASURE OF FAITH THAT GOD HAS ASSIGNED."

W hen we seek to understand the teaching of Scripture, probably the most important principle to keep in mind is that Scripture interprets itself. No one biblical passage can be accurately understood in isolation from others, and this has been recognized from the days of the early church to the present. If our interpretation of one text would force us to deny the plain meaning of another passage, then we have interpreted God's Word incorrectly.

At first glance, a text such as Titus 2:11 might appear to state that every individual has an equal opportunity to be saved, since Paul says that the grace of God has appeared to all people. This is the position that Arminians and Wesleyans take; it must be rejected, however, in light of the rest of Scripture. Given Jesus' promise that no one whom the Father draws will fail to come to Him (John 6:35–47), saving grace must not be offered to all people. If it were, then everyone would be saved, for everyone would be drawn by the Father to His Son, Jesus Christ. But since everyone is not in fact a believer in Christ, and since some have been passed over for salvation and will end up in hell (Matt. 26:24; Rom. 9:19–24; 1 Peter 2:8), we understand that Titus 2:11 cannot be teaching that all people have an opportunity for salvation. The text must mean that all kinds of people, not every individual, receive saving grace.

II

DAY 34 & 35

Arminians and Wesleyans may be wrong that all people have an equal opportunity for salvation, but at least they believe that God's grace must do something in order for people to be redeemed. This was not so for Charles Grandison Finney, one of the most important religious leaders in nineteenth-century America. Although Finney is esteemed by many people in the church today, he was actually a thoroughgoing Pelagian who believed that human beings are morally capable of choosing Christ. Grace is unnecessary, for human beings can develop the right frame of mind to believe in Jesus. It is the job of the preacher to do whatever he can to help get people into the right emotional and mental state to believe in Jesus. Finney's legacy lives on in the modern church's emphasis on using manipulative methods to produce professions of faith in Christ.

FOR FURTHER STUDY

Isaiah 55:10-11; 1 Corinthians 1:18-31

Finney and those who believe in human ability are guilty of violating Romans 12:3. They think of themselves—indeed, of all people—more highly than they should, giving them an ability that Scripture does not say they possess. Moreover, they trust in their own power, not the power of God's Word, to save, ultimately denying God the glory He's due.

APPLICATION

The power of God for conversion is in His grace working through the preaching of the gospel (1 Cor. 1:21). We do not have to invent fancy techniques to bring people to faith; we just have to preach God's Word accurately and trust Him to save His people. Let us put our hope not in methods but in faithfulness to God's Word.

III

WORSHIP

In worship, we draw near to the triune God in reverence and awe, praising Him for His glorious character and gracious works. This section explores biblical worship in the Christian life, examining how we are to worship God according to what He has revealed in His Word.

Worship is fundamental to the Creator-creation relationship, and the failure to worship God reveals the corruption of humankind (Rom. 1:21, 25). Yet for those who are the recipients of God's saving grace, worship empowered by the Spirit of God is our fitting and appropriate response to His kindness and favor toward us in Christ (Rom. 12:1).

Worship can be well summarized in the command given to Israel after the exodus and expanded on by Jesus during His earthly ministry: "You shall love the Lord your God with all your heart and with all your soul and with all your might" (Deut. 6:5; see Matt. 22:37-40). Worship from such a heart is acceptable to God when its practice is governed by His Word.

The practice of worship includes not only our private worship of the Lord as individuals as we read and meditate on Scripture and offer praise and thanks to God, but also our corporate worship in the church as together we sing, pray, receive His Word, and participate in the sacraments.

REDEEMED TO WORSHIP

EXODUS 3:18 "YOU AND THE ELDERS OF ISRAEL SHALL GO TO THE KING OF EGYPT AND SAY TO HIM, 'THE LORD, THE GOD OF THE HEBREWS, HAS MET WITH US; AND NOW, PLEASE LET US GO A THREE DAYS' JOURNEY INTO THE WILDERNESS, THAT WE MAY SACRIFICE TO THE LORD OUR GOD.'"

W orship is the chief reason for our existence. The answer to the first question of the Westminster Shorter Catechism is that our chief end is to glorify God and to enjoy Him forever. We were made to worship the Lord, and we fulfill our purpose for living when we worship Him. Scripture teaches us this in various ways. For example, when Paul surveys the condition of fallen human beings in Romans 1:18–3:20, he notes that the result of sin is that people exchange the worship of the one true God for the worship of created things. Worship is so integral to what it means to be human that we cannot help but serve and praise something. It is not that we will cease worship altogether if we reject the Creator; rather, we will go on worshiping but change the object of our worship—to our great peril.

We also see worship ordained in the account of creation. The Lord set apart the seventh day as holy and rested on that day (Gen. 2:1–3). Later, in Deuteronomy 5:12–15, we read God's calling of His people to remember His great acts of salvation. On that seventh day, remembering what God has done is part of worship, and even if there had never been a fall, we would have a Sabbath rest where we would recall what the Lord has done in creation.

Finally, that God saves us for the purpose of worshiping Him reveals worship as the supreme end to which we are called. In today's passage, we read of how the Lord told Moses to go to Pharaoh and command the king to free the Israelites so that they could sacrifice to God—so that they could worship Him (Ex. 3:18). God's intent in saving His people is to create a community of worshipers who praise Him in spirit and in truth (John 4:23).

FOR
FURTHER
STUDY

Exodus
20:1-3;
1 Peter
2:9

Human beings were made to worship God, and they experience true fulfillment only as they live as worshipers of our triune Creator. Worship is not incidental—it is the reason for our existence. As you go to worship this next Lord's Day, remember that in praising the God who made you, you are fulfilling your purpose for existence.

DAY 37

GUIDANCE IN WORSHIP

ROMANS 1:18-23 "CLAIMING TO BE WISE, [HUMAN BEINGS] BECAME FOOLS, AND EXCHANGED THE GLORY OF THE IMMORTAL GOD FOR IMAGES RESEMBLING MORTAL MAN AND BIRDS AND ANIMALS AND CREEPING THINGS" (VV. 22-23).

H uman beings, we have seen, are worshipers by nature. Our fallenness, however, means that not every idea we have about worship is going to be a sound one. Our natural propensity apart from divine grace, as seen in Romans 1:18–23, is to engage in explicit idolatry. Yet passages such as 1 John 5:21 that warn Christians to keep themselves from idols show us that it is at least possible for believers to introduce idolatrous practices into the worship of the one true God. Clearly, we need guidance on how to worship the Lord rightly.

Thankfully, our Lord provides such direction in His Word. In summarizing the key Reformed teaching on worship, Westminster Confession of Faith 21.1 states, "The acceptable way of worshiping the true God is instituted by himself." When we look for guidance as to how we are to worship God, we turn to Scripture, for the Word of God is our only infallible guide to faith and life, and in His Word, God has given us the key principles that reveal what is pleasing to Him in worship.

Where do we find these principles in Scripture? Of course, nearly every book in the Bible touches on what it means to worship the Lord properly, but books such as Exodus, Leviticus,

III

DAY 36 & 37

FOR
FURTHER
STUDY
___
Leviticus
10:1-3;
Deuteron-
omy 12;
John 4:24;
Romans
12:1-2

and Psalms in particular give us much guidance for what God-honoring worship looks like. Now, at this point we should note that applying the principles found in Scripture is not always easy, and there have been disagreements over how these principles should be applied even within the Reformed tradition. Nevertheless, we cannot go far wrong if we seek to do in worship only that which has biblical warrant or what by good and necessary consequence can be deduced as being in harmony with scriptural principles.

APPLICATION

Over the past few decades, we have seen many silly and irreverent things introduced into worship in order to draw a crowd and keep people entertained. To do such things, however, is to play with fire. We must follow God's prescriptions for worship. We risk offering false worship to God when we do not follow His inspired directions for how to praise Him.

DAY 38

REVERENT WORSHIP

LEVITICUS 10:1-3 "MOSES SAID TO AARON, 'THIS IS WHAT THE LORD HAS SAID: "AMONG THOSE WHO ARE NEAR ME I WILL BE SANCTIFIED, AND BEFORE ALL THE PEOPLE I WILL BE GLORIFIED."' AND AARON HELD HIS PEACE" (V. 3).

L eviticus functioned as a manual for the ancient Israelites regarding the offering of sacrifices and other elements of worship. Although Christ has fulfilled the old covenant sacrifices, there is still much that we as new covenant believers can learn from Leviticus about how God is to be worshiped. The story of Nadab and Abihu found in today's passage certainly ranks as one of the most important lessons about worship.

Nadab and Abihu were sons of Aaron and thus part of the old covenant priesthood tasked with leading the worship of God's people. Sadly for them, on one occasion they offered "unauthorized fire" before the Lord (Lev. 10:1). In recounting this story,

Moses does not tell us of what this unauthorized fire consisted. It could have been fire offered at the wrong time, fire made with the wrong combination of spices, or something else. What is most important about this unapproved fire is that it was fire that God "had not commanded them" (v. 1). Nadab and Abihu took it upon themselves to worship our Creator in a way that was against what He commanded, and the result was their deaths (v. 2).

This text supports the idea that our worship must be in agreement with divinely revealed principles. Moreover, it stresses the importance of reverence in worship. We are to come before the Lord with a reverent attitude, remembering who He is and who we are. But our intent to worship God reverently means little if we worship Him contrary to His commands. To show true reverence to God is to remember that He is the Lawgiver, and those who are truly reverent will do whatever He commands, not adding to it or subtracting from it (Deut. 4:2).

Leviticus 10:3 captures the importance of reverence in thought and action in our worship. God must be sanctified before His people by those who lead in the worship of the Creator. John Calvin, in his commentary on today's passage, stresses the importance of worshiping rightly in thought and deed. He suggests that Nadab and Abihu did not intend to be irreverent but that they actually were irreverent by not worshiping according to God's prescriptions. We may think we are doing well, but if a particular worship practice is contrary to biblical principles, we are in danger of offending the Lord and reaping disastrous consequences. Irreverent worship can lead to death even under the new covenant (1 Cor. 11:27–30), so we must take care to worship God reverently according to His Word.

FOR FURTHER STUDY

Leviticus 19:30; Psalm 89:5-18; Hebrews 5:7; 12:28-29

APPLICATION

Strikingly absent from much of Christian worship today is an atmosphere of reverence that takes God seriously and seeks to glorify Him according to His Word. Much of this is due to the fact that we have downplayed the holiness of God and the lordship of Christ in the covenant community. As you attend worship, endeavor to remember who God is and to approach Him with reverent thanks for His goodness to you.

III

DAY 37 & 38

WORSHIPING IN SPIRIT AND TRUTH

JOHN 4:24 "GOD IS SPIRIT, AND THOSE WHO WORSHIP HIM
MUST WORSHIP IN SPIRIT AND TRUTH."

J esus' encounter with the Samaritan woman as recorded
in John's gospel is one of the most instructive passages of
Scripture on the topic of worship. The Samaritans were
the descendants of the ancient northern kingdom of Israel who
had intermarried with non-Israelites that the Assyrian Empire
settled in the promised land after 722 BC. By the time of Jesus'
earthly ministry, these Samaritans had developed a distinct theology, believing that the true place of worship was Mount Gerizim
and following a version of the five books of Moses (Genesis–Deuteronomy) edited to reflect that belief.

This information forms an important backdrop to our Lord's
comments that God is seeking worshipers who worship "in spirit
and truth" (John 4:24). The Samaritans were not worshiping God
in truth, for they had altered God's Word and were not offering
sacrifices in the true designated place for sacrifice—the temple
on Mount Zion. Yes, Jesus was soon to fulfill the temple's purpose
and establish an order in which worship could be offered elsewhere (vv. 20–23), but that had not yet happened when He spoke
to the Samaritan woman. Our Savior's words, therefore, served as
an implicit critique of Samaritan practices and all worship not
regulated by God's Word. Dr. R.C. Sproul writes in his commentary *John*: "Our worship must be based on God's self-revelation
in Scripture. He is truth and His Word is truth."

In addressing the Samaritan woman, Christ also spoke of spiritual worship. He said that those who worship God must "worship
in *spirit* and truth." What does this mean? First, note how worship
in spirit is combined with worship in truth. This tells us that we
cannot have one without the other. Whatever else it may be, worship that is not conducted according to the truth of God's Word
is not worship in spirit.

John Calvin's comments on this text explain what it means

to worship God in spirit: "The worship of God is said to consist in the spirit, because it is nothing else than that inward faith of the heart which produces prayer, and, next, purity of conscience and self-denial, that we may be dedicated to obedience to God as holy sacrifices." To worship God in spirit is to worship Him with the right spirit—to worship Him in true faith that believes what He says and that He rewards those who seek Him (Heb. 11:6). In other words, worship in spirit is not worship that merely goes through the motions. To worship in spirit is to set our hearts and minds on the Lord when we praise Him.

FOR
FURTHER
STUDY

1 Samuel
15:22;
Psalms
19:14;
24:3-4;
51:17;
64:10;
86:12; Phi-
lippians
3:3

APPLICATION

Dr. Sproul also comments on today's passage that Jesus exhorts us "to see that the worship we offer comes from the depths of our souls, from our inner spirits, from the very cores of our being." There will be an outward form to our worship, but it must not be dead formalism. In worship, we must give to God all that we are, loving and glorifying Him with all our heart, soul, mind, and strength.

`DAY 40`

THE PLACE OF WORSHIP

JOHN 4:20-23 "JESUS SAID TO [THE SAMARITAN WOMAN], 'WOMAN, BELIEVE ME, THE HOUR IS COMING WHEN NEITHER ON THIS MOUNTAIN NOR IN JERUSALEM WILL YOU WORSHIP THE FATHER. . . . BUT THE HOUR IS COMING, AND IS NOW HERE, WHEN THE TRUE WORSHIPERS WILL WORSHIP THE FATHER IN SPIRIT AND TRUTH, FOR THE FATHER IS SEEK-ING SUCH PEOPLE TO WORSHIP HIM'" (VV. 21-23).

III

Animal sacrifices constituted a major part of old covenant worship, and the place where these sacrifices could be offered was highly regulated by God. Following the settlement of Israel in the promised land, the Israelites were supposed to seek the Lord for the place they were to bring their

DAY 39 & 40

burnt offerings and sacrifices (Deut. 12:5–7), and God revealed to David that the temple and altar were to be built in Jerusalem (1 Chron. 21:1–22:1). After the construction of the temple, anyone who offered sacrifices at other places violated the Lord's will, and the books of 1 and 2 Kings frequently condemn kings who built altars elsewhere, even if they were altars to the God of Israel.

This establishment of a central sanctuary for sacrifice does not mean that the old covenant saints could not worship God at all outside Jerusalem. Jesus' participation in the synagogue services in Nazareth, for example, shows us that God approved of the singing, prayers, instruction, and other acts of worship conducted at those local meeting places (Luke 4:16–27). Still, Jerusalem remained the only place where the Jews could lawfully offer sacrifices to God.

Under the new covenant, things have changed. No longer is there one sanctuary to which all believers are obliged to go for worshiping the Lord. Since Jesus has fulfilled the temple and its sacrificial system (Heb. 9–10), there is no need for a central place of worship. Jesus told the Samaritan woman that a day was coming when people would worship not in Jerusalem or on Mount Gerizim but elsewhere and that such worship would be acceptable as long as it was conducted in spirit and truth (John 4:20–23). Of course, people were supposed to worship God in spirit and truth under the old covenant, but worshiping in truth then meant offering animal sacrifices only in Jerusalem.

In any case, today there is no single location where all Christians must go for corporate worship. Duly established churches may meet for worship in homes, in movie theaters, in school lunchrooms, on the seashore, or in any other location. That is

FOR
FURTHER
STUDY
—
Nehemiah 1;
Acts 16:13;
Colossians
4:15; Rev-
elation
1:9-10

not to say that creating dedicated sanctuaries for worship is prohibited. There is, in fact, great wisdom in building sanctuaries of beauty where the church can gather to worship God, and church sanctuaries at their best help us focus our hearts and minds on the Lord in worship. But they are not absolutely required. True worship happens wherever we praise God in spirit and in truth (John 4:24).

Some Christians frown on the practice of building sanctuaries for worship. Yet while church buildings are not required, worship is, and a designated place for worship enables people to be more conscious of God's presence and their need to revere Him. Because worship is so important, we should support our churches as they endeavor to create spaces where we can worship God in spirit, truth, and beauty.

DAY 41

THE TIME OF WORSHIP

REVELATION 1:10 "I WAS IN THE SPIRIT ON THE LORD'S DAY, AND I HEARD BEHIND ME A LOUD VOICE LIKE A TRUMPET."

Drive in an area where many Seventh-day Adventists live and you might see bumper stickers that say something like "Sunday is *not* the Sabbath" or "God chose the seventh day for the Sabbath and never changed His mind." For Seventh-day Adventists and others who worship on Saturday, the seventh day of the week, gathering for worship on Sunday is sin because there is no command in Scripture to worship on the first day of the week.

We can appreciate that these groups want to follow only what God says in the Bible, but we must disagree that the proper time for worship is only the seventh day. Our Reformation doctrine of Scripture is that we believe both what the Word tells us explicitly and what it teaches by good and necessary consequence (Westminster Confession of Faith 1.6). This Reformation view comes from Jesus Himself, who deduced the doctrine of the resurrection from the Mosaic law when confronting the Sadducees (Matt. 22:23–33). Scripture may teach something without giving us an explicit statement on the subject. We believe that there is one God in three persons not because there is an explicit three-in-one statement in the Bible but because the Trinity is a good and necessary deduction from the whole of biblical revelation.

III

DAY 40 & 41

As we look at Scripture's teaching on the Sabbath, we find a stress on a seven-day cycle of work and rest. In fact, one rationale for the fourth commandment is that God worked on six days in creation and rested on one day, the seventh day (Ex. 20:8–11). Preserving this cycle seems to be one of the key purposes of this commandment, so any change in this era of redemptive history would have to preserve this cycle.

Also, ancient Israel, on the Sabbath day, celebrated the key redemptive act of the old covenant—namely, the exodus from Egypt (Deut. 5:12–15). Surely, then, we should set aside a day on which to commemorate the key redemptive act of the new covenant—and in all history—namely, Christ's resurrection, which took place on the first day of the week (Matt. 28:1–10). The Apostles set the first day aside, as revealed in places such as Revelation 1:10 and Acts 20:7. So we have Apostolic precedent for changing the Sabbath from the seventh day to the first day while preserving the seven-day cycle of work, worship, and rest.

FOR
FURTHER
STUDY
—
Numbers
28:16-25;
1 Corinthi-
ans 16:1-4

Consequently, we have ample warrant for setting aside Sunday as the time of obligatory Christian worship. Unless prevented by tasks necessary for the health and welfare of others, we must gather with other believers for worship on the first day of each week.

APPLICATION

Churches may establish other nonobligatory days of worship and celebration besides the first day of the week. But the only Christian day of worship that must be observed is the Lord's Day. Let us take our responsibility to worship and rest on the Lord's Day seriously and make the most of our corporate gatherings every week.

DAY 42

HEAVENLY WORSHIP

HEBREWS 12:18-28 "YOU HAVE COME TO MOUNT ZION AND TO THE CITY OF THE LIVING GOD, THE HEAVENLY JERUSALEM, AND TO INNUMERABLE ANGELS IN FESTAL GATHERING, AND TO THE ASSEMBLY OF THE FIRSTBORN WHO ARE ENROLLED

IN HEAVEN, AND TO GOD, THE JUDGE OF ALL, AND TO THE
SPIRITS OF THE RIGHTEOUS MADE PERFECT, AND TO JESUS,
THE MEDIATOR OF A NEW COVENANT" (VV. 22-24).

J ohn 4:20–24 tells us that God seeks worshipers who will
worship Him in spirit and truth. In our devotionals on
that text, we noted that among other things, the passage
explains that there is no central place where all Christians are
obligated to offer worship under the new covenant. Yet we must
now qualify this assertion slightly. Actually, John 4:20–24 reveals
that there is no single earthly location where we must gather for
worship. But when we look at worship from a heavenly perspec-
tive, we see something different.

We are talking about the reality that no matter where we gather
with God's people on this earth, we are actually at the same time
in heaven worshiping God. As Dr. R.C. Sproul often stated, when
we enter into worship, we cross the threshold from the secular to
the sacred, from the common to the holy. And this means more
than just setting apart an earthly gathering place. Christian worship takes place simultaneously on an earthly and a heavenly
plane. Though it is not normally discernible to our five senses,
heaven and earth come together when we join with God's people in worship.

Today's passage is one of several texts that support this belief.
Hebrews 12:18–24 is not only about worship, for it appears in
the immediate context of encouraging us to press on as we run the
race of faith in our earthly lives (see vv. 1–17). Nevertheless, the
passage certainly assumes our worship in heaven. In speaking
of our coming to "the spirits of the righteous made perfect" and
"the heavenly Jerusalem," the author clearly has in view our entry
into God's presence in the heavenly temple. And we can connect
this with worship both in the text itself—verse 28 points us to
the offering of acceptable worship—and in the larger context of
Hebrews. After all, the author encourages us to draw near to the
throne of grace where Jesus, our Great High Priest, intercedes
for us (4:14–16). But where is the throne of grace besides heaven
itself, and how do we draw near except through prayer, which is

III

DAY 41 & 42

an act of worship? Clearly, there is a heavenly reality in which we participate when we worship God.

FOR
FURTHER
STUDY

We should also mention Paul's comment in 1 Corinthians 11:10. Women should have their heads covered in worship "because of the angels." This enigmatic statement continues to confound interpreters, but surely it is not a stretch to suggest that we may infer from it that we are worshiping alongside the angels in heaven when we join with others to praise God.

2 Kings
6:15-17;
Psalm 11:4;
Hebrews
9:24; Rev-
elation 21

APPLICATION

That our worship takes place simultaneously in heaven and on earth has ramifications for how we plan and conduct worship. Our worship should be worthy of heaven itself and should reflect the things that are valued in heaven—sincerity, truth, beauty, dignity, and so forth. We will avoid much impiety and silliness in worship if we remember that we are actually worshiping in heaven every Lord's Day.

DAY 43

READING SCRIPTURE IN WORSHIP

1 TIMOTHY 4:13 "UNTIL I COME, DEVOTE YOURSELF TO THE PUBLIC READING OF SCRIPTURE."

We are not free to do anything in worship; rather, the Lord is to be worshiped according to what Scripture reveals. And the biblical principles for God-honoring worship are discerned by applying sound rules of interpretation to God's Word.

There are many elements that Scripture prescribes for our worship. The first of these is the public reading of the Scriptures, which Paul exhorts Timothy to practice in today's passage. Although for Timothy, this reading aloud of the Scriptures in worship would have consisted mainly of Old Testament readings, since the New Testament had not yet been completed, the imperative applies to the entire Bible. In short, all worship services should include readings from the Bible.

Reading the Scriptures aloud in worship has several advantages. First, it helps the congregation become more acquainted with the content of the Word of God. Second, reading the Bible aloud to God's people guarantees that they will hear divine truth. Even if the preacher has an off week or inadvertently delivers a mistaken teaching, having the Scriptures read aloud in the service ensures that the Lord's flock receives God's truth and can be encouraged to heed it. Third, it is also worth noting that the Scriptures have been designed to be read aloud. During the period in which the Scriptures were written, very few people could read, and even those who could read seldom owned their own copies of any portion of the Bible. They learned the Word of God by hearing it. We are blessed in our day that most adults, at least in the West, can read and that we can even own our own Bibles and bring them to church. But that is a recent phenomenon. God gave His Word not only for us to read in private but for us to hear it read aloud, and if in His divine wisdom He gave it for reading aloud, we are missing something if Scripture is not read publicly in worship.

From the earliest history of God's people, the covenant community has gathered to hear God's Word read aloud (Deut. 31:10–13). May we be eager to hear it read during worship in our day.

2 Kings
22:8-23:27;
Nehemiah
9:1-3; Acts
13:13-15;
Colossians
4:16

APPLICATION

We are certainly blessed to be able to read along in our own Bibles with our pastors as they read Scripture aloud during worship. There is also benefit in our hearing the Word of God read to us even when we do not have a Bible in front of us. God works through the reading of His Word to instruct us, so let us take advantage of any opportunity we have to hear God's Word read to us.

III

DAY 44

EXHORTATION AND TEACHING IN WORSHIP

DAY 43 & 44

1 TIMOTHY 4:13 "UNTIL I COME, DEVOTE YOURSELF . . .
TO EXHORTATION, TO TEACHING."

S cholars of religion often note the importance of words for the Christian religion. We define orthodox theology with words, and the words of our prayers and songs express our piety. But the importance of words for biblical religion is most evident in our reliance on the written Word of God. Ever since the days of Moses, the reading of the Scriptures has been definitional for the religion of God's people, and as 1 Timothy 4:13 indicates, the public reading of Scripture must be a part of our worship services.

Yet 1 Timothy 4:13 says more about the Scriptures in worship than that we are to read them aloud. Paul also tells Timothy and, by extension, all Christian pastors to be devoted to exhortation and to teaching. There is, in fact, a careful sequence laid out in today's passage. First the Word of God is to be read, and then it is to be explained. John Calvin comments, "[Paul] places reading before doctrine and exhortation; for, undoubtedly, the Scripture is the fountain of all wisdom, from which pastors must draw all that they place before their flock."

Pastors and teachers have nothing to give to God's people besides what the Lord has given—namely, His inspired Word. Thus, essential to worship is exhortation and teaching based on that Word. The word "teaching," or in some translations "doctrine," has in view the systematic exposition and explanation of Scripture for the purpose of establishing what we are to believe. "Exhortation" refers more to the practical application of the text to God's people. Those who teach God's Word in the worship service are to explain and apply it, helping us learn how to love our Creator more truly and follow Him more rightly.

Scripture is clear enough that anyone can read it and discern the basic message of salvation. But some portions of the Bible are harder to understand than others, and so God has given the church teachers to help us learn His Word and grow in grace and truth (Eph. 4:11–14). Because the Word is essential to our lives as Christians and because God has given us pastors, elders, and teachers to assist us in bringing this Word to bear on our lives, Christian worship conducted according to the Bible will always involve the teaching of the Bible.

Pastors, elders, and teachers must place a high priority on studying the Bible so that they may rightly proclaim it to their congregations. But laypeople are responsible as well to call on their leaders to teach them God's Word. Let us encourage our pastors, elders, and teachers to give us the Word of God in our worship.

FOR FURTHER STUDY

Nehemiah 8:1-8; Acts 2:42; 2 Timothy 3:16-17; 4:1-2

APPLICATION

If God's people do not call for their pastors, elders, and teachers to bring them the Word, their leaders may be tempted to give them something different. We are all responsible to make sure that God's Word is faithfully proclaimed. If we are teachers, then we must take care to exposit the Word carefully. If we are laity, we must ask for the Word to be preached in our congregations and listen when it is.

DAY 45

PRAYER IN WORSHIP

ACTS 2:42 "THEY DEVOTED THEMSELVES TO THE APOSTLES' TEACHING AND . . . THE PRAYERS."

I f our goal in worship is to worship only according to the Lord's prescriptions, we can hardly do better than to look at how those through whom God revealed His Word—the Apostles and prophets—worshiped. Acts 2:42 features our earliest record of the church's worship after Pentecost, and it sets before us several essential elements of worship.

First, note that the earliest Christians devoted themselves "to the apostles' teaching." This practice confirms what we have said about the importance of reading and teaching the Word of God in our worship services, for the Apostles' teaching comes to us today only in the canonical Scriptures.

Second and more important for our devotional today is that during the Apostolic period, the early church was devoted to "the prayers." The early church was a praying church, and prayers

III

were an integral part of early Christian worship. This is not surprising. After all, the first Christians were mostly of a Jewish background, and prayers were an important part of synagogue worship. Moreover, prayers were also offered to God during worship conducted at the temple in Jerusalem. Notably, Solomon prayed at the temple's dedication (1 Kings 8), but prayer was also a regular part of daily temple worship. For example, the people confessed their sins when they brought their sacrifices (Lev. 5:1–6). Of course, the book of Psalms is itself a prayer book, and many of the psalms were written specifically for use in public worship. Several of them were for "the choirmaster" (for example, Ps. 61), and public worship was the occasion for the choir to sing (2 Chron. 29:25–30).

Speaking of the book of Psalms, it is under the category of prayer that singing finds its place in Christian worship. The various psalms were sung prayers, and it is right to sing unto the Lord under the new covenant as well. Singing can also fall under the category of teaching in worship. Paul writes in Colossians 3:16 that we are to teach and admonish "one another in all wisdom, singing psalms and hymns and spiritual songs, with thankfulness in [our] hearts to God." We may not always remember this, but our hymns and songs are vehicles for proclaiming God's truth and thus can serve a teaching function as well as the function of prayer as we offer them with thankful hearts to the Lord. Prayers both spoken and sung are essential in biblically faithful worship.

FOR
FURTHER
STUDY
───
2 Chron-
icles
29:25-30;
Psalm 5;
Romans
12:12;
1 Timothy
2:1-2

APPLICATION

We often think of prayer as a spiritual discipline for private worship and devotion, and so it is. But prayer is also a public devotion that is to be a part of corporate worship. When we sing hymns or pray in unison, let us do so with our hearts and minds fully engaged. And during the pastoral prayer, let us think carefully on the pastor's words and ask the Lord for the prayer to be answered.

DAY 46

SACRAMENTS IN WORSHIP

ACTS 2:42 "AND THEY DEVOTED THEMSELVES . . . TO THE
BREAKING OF BREAD."

A cts 2:42 provides our most important look at the earliest
practices of the Apostolic church. We have seen that when
the first Christians came together for worship, they were
committed to "the apostles' teaching." This would have encom-
passed both the Apostles' teaching of the old covenant Scriptures
and any new revelation given by Christ that would eventually
be set in writing. Thus we see how important the teaching and
preaching of God's Word were for Apostolic worship. Acts 2:42
also reveals that the earliest Christians devoted themselves to "the
prayers." Undoubtedly this would have included prayers from the
book of Psalms, for the first believers were from a Jewish background, and probably the Lord's Prayer and prayers patterned after
it, for that is how Jesus taught the Apostles to pray (Matt. 6:9–13).

In addition to teaching and prayer, we see in Acts 2:42 that the
Apostles also administered the sacraments during worship. They
were devoted "to the breaking of bread." There would be little
reason for Luke (the author of the book of Acts) to tell us that the
believers ate ordinary meals together, so the specific mention of
bread is almost certainly a reference to the Lord's Supper. Given
what we know of early Christian worship, it is likely that the Lord's
Supper was enjoyed as part of a larger fellowship meal. In any
case, 1 Corinthians 11:17–34 makes it plain that the Lord's Supper
was a part of the worship of the church during the Apostolic era.

That the sacraments would be ordained for public worship
makes sense given what Scripture says about them. The command to baptize, for example, is given alongside the command
that we teach all nations to observe all that Christ has instructed
us (Matt. 28:18–20). The teaching and preaching of Christ's commandments occur in public worship, so ordinarily, baptism should

III

DAY 45 & 46

as well. From both the institution of the Lord's Supper (26:26–29) and Paul's description of its practice in 1 Corinthians 11, we see that partaking of the bread and wine was never a private act but rather something done publicly with other disciples.

FOR
FURTHER
STUDY
⎯⎯⎯
Mark 14:22-
25; Luke
3:1-22

Baptism and the Lord's Supper complement other aspects of worship. They are visible depictions of gospel truths proclaimed as the Word of God is taught that reinforce the preached message and are explained by it. In the sacraments, we also meet with Christ, and meeting with the triune God is one of the purposes of worship.

APPLICATION

In today's church, some Christians believe that the sacraments can be a private affair, that it is right to take the Lord's Supper in the privacy of one's home apart from public worship. Scripture shows us otherwise. The sacraments are public ordinances, and we participate in them rightly in the context of public worship. Let us encourage our leaders to place a high value on the public administration of baptism and the Lord's Supper.

DAY 47

OATHS AND VOWS IN WORSHIP

NEHEMIAH 10:28-29 "THE REST OF THE PEOPLE . . . JOIN WITH THEIR BROTHERS, THEIR NOBLES, AND ENTER INTO A CURSE AND AN OATH TO WALK IN GOD'S LAW THAT WAS GIVEN BY MOSES THE SERVANT OF GOD, AND TO OBSERVE AND DO ALL THE COMMANDMENTS OF THE Lord OUR LORD AND HIS RULES AND HIS STATUTES."

T oday we come to a subject that many people have misunderstood: oaths and vows. Among the various elements that constitute Christian worship, Westminster Confession of Faith 21.5 includes the swearing of lawful oaths and vows. This has been a contentious topic for many Christians because of certain passages that seem at first glance to prohibit the taking of oaths and vows by believers. For example, Matthew 5:33–37 records Jesus' teaching that we should "not take an oath at all."

A careful consideration of Matthew's text, however, shows us that Jesus was not outlawing all oaths and vows. Instead, He was correcting a common Jewish belief that if you swear an oath by anything other than God's name, you are not obliged to fulfill the oath. Jesus' point is that swearing an oath by heaven, Jerusalem, or any other thing does not release someone from keeping the oath. As long as it is a lawful oath, it is made in the presence of God the Creator even when His name is not invoked. Thus, the Lord will hold us accountable. Jesus was teaching that it is better not to swear an oath at all if you are looking for a way out of keeping it.

Apostolic practice confirms that Jesus did not intend to abolish oath-taking altogether. For example, Acts 18:18 tells us that the Apostle Paul made vows even after he was converted to Christ. This should not surprise us, for the practice of swearing vows was commonplace for Jews such as Paul. The Old Testament records several occasions on which the people swore vows in the context of worship. During one celebration of the Feast of Booths, for instance, the postexilic community took vows to keep the law of God, as we read in today's passage (Neh. 10:28–29). We also read of a similar vow that the people of Israel took at the point of the initial ratification of the Mosaic covenant (Ex. 24).

The Westminster Confession closely associates oaths and vows with special occasions, which makes sense given that the Old Testament examples of oaths above took place during festivals and other infrequent or special observances. We should note, however, that in one sense, every worship service is itself an oath or vow. Every Lord's Day, we come before God with praise, confessing our sin, testifying that we are His people, and recommitting ourselves to serving Him in the week ahead of us.

FOR FURTHER STUDY

Leviticus 27; Numbers 6:1–21; Psalm 65:1; Hebrews 6:16

III

DAY 46 & 47

APPLICATION

Worship in the Reformed tradition has often been seen as a service of covenant renewal, and in Scripture vows are taken when the covenant is renewed (see Josh. 24). Our worship itself can be seen as a vow to serve God. That is one of the reasons why it should be taken seriously. Worship is a holy occasion on which we meet with our holy God to swear allegiance to Him. It is not a time for frivolity.

FASTING IN WORSHIP

JOEL 2:12 "'YET EVEN NOW,' DECLARES THE LORD, 'RETURN TO ME WITH ALL YOUR HEART, WITH FASTING, WITH WEEPING, AND WITH MOURNING.'"

U nder the new covenant, corporate worship takes place primarily on the Lord's Day, since that is when the Apostles gathered with the early Christians to remember the great salvation purchased by Christ (Acts 20:7). That does not mean, however, that corporate worship should never take place at other times. Significant streams of the Reformed tradition have long recognized that the church may call for corporate worship on other days as long as these special occasions of worship are not made obligatory. Even the Westminster Confession, which represents a current of Reformed thought that was most reluctant to encourage the celebration of special worship services on Christmas Day and other traditional feast days, recognizes that a church has liberty to call for special occasions of worship outside the weekly observance of the Lord's Day. On such occasions of worship, we must do only what is in accord with biblical principles.

Some of the special occasions that Westminster Confession 21.5 suggests may be appropriate at times are "solemn fastings." Often, we think of fasting as an individual discipline, but Scripture clearly has a place for corporate fasts as well. Today's passage, for example, records God's calling to the old covenant community to repent and fast so as to avoid divine judgment (Joel 2:12). Ezra called for fasting and prayer for the Lord's protection when he was leading the people back to the promised land (Ezra 8:21–23). In the New Testament, we read of the church at Antioch worshiping and fasting just before setting apart Barnabas and Saul for their missionary work (Acts 13:1–3).

We see, then, that fasting can be a part of public worship no less than it can be observed in private worship (Matt. 6:16–18). But why would we fast? It cannot be to somehow merit an answer to prayer, for we do not earn God's favor by depriving ourselves of His good gifts. Instead, fasting can serve as a reminder to pray. As we feel pangs of hunger, we are reminded of our commitment to set aside time during which we would normally be eating in order to pray for a particular person or situation that inspired the fast to begin with. Fasting also reminds us of our creatureliness and dependence. We are ever tempted to believe that we are self-sufficient, but the hunger we experience in fasting helps us recall that we are needy creatures. That, in turn, drives us to more conscious dependence on God and His blessings.

FOR FURTHER STUDY

Isaiah 58; Daniel 9:1-23; Matthew 6:16-18; Acts 14:19-23

APPLICATION

Although there can be occasions on which corporate fasting is appropriate, fasting is primarily a personal discipline. When we fast, we are driven to more urgent prayer and to remember our creaturely dependence. If you have not fasted before, consider whether you should fast and pray this week.

DAY 49

THANKSGIVING IN WORSHIP

ESTHER 9:20-22 "THEY SHOULD MAKE THEM DAYS OF FEAST-ING AND GLADNESS, DAYS FOR SENDING GIFTS OF FOOD TO ONE ANOTHER AND GIFTS TO THE POOR" (V. 22).

H aman, the inveterate enemy of the Jews during the Persian period, once attempted to annihilate the Jewish people (Est. 3:7–11). In the providence of God, he ultimately failed because of the intervention of Esther and Mordecai, and the Jews actually "gained mastery over those who hated them" (9:1). To commemorate the rescue of the Jews, the feast of Purim was established

III

DAY 48 & 49

(vv. 20–22). To this day, observant Jews keep the feast of Purim by sending gifts to one another and retelling the story of Esther.

Westminster Confession of Faith 21.5 cites the establishment of Purim in Esther 9:20–22 as support in asserting that the church may at times call for special occasions of thanksgiving outside of weekly Lord's Day worship. Thus, we see that Scripture allows for services of thanksgiving for the covenant community, and we see that today, many Reformed churches mark significant events with public gatherings for expressing gratitude. Some churches hold services of thanksgiving to celebrate paying off the mortgage on the church building. Others might hold them in conjunction with a national holiday such as Thanksgiving Day. Some churches even have thanksgiving services to recognize their pastors or a church anniversary. Truly, there are many times when a special worship service of thanksgiving can be appropriate.

Yet while the Westminster Confession describes thanksgiving on special occasions, it does not mean that thanksgiving should not be a part of ordinary, weekly worship. If one of the chief failures of unredeemed humanity is failing to give God thanks (Rom. 1:21), then surely the worship of the redeemed should be full of expressions of gratitude for the Lord's provision of salvation and our daily needs. Moreover, Paul assumes that Christian worship will include expressions of thanksgiving, for he calls for believers not to utter their thanks in tongues but to do so in the common language (1 Cor. 14:13–19).

FOR
FURTHER
STUDY

———

1 Chron-
icles
16:8–36;
Philippi-
ans 4:6;
Colossians
4:2; Rev-
elation
11:15–19

Because we have received the undeserved gift of God's grace in Christ, we who believe in Jesus ought to be the most grateful of all people. This means that we should thank our Creator regularly, both as private individuals and as a body during worship. Thanking God for who He is and what He has done expresses our awareness of who the Lord is—our sovereign, gracious Maker—and who we are as undeserving creatures who have been brought into a saving relationship with Him.

APPLICATION

Most of our regular worship services include expressions of thanksgiving to God for His redemption. We should participate in these wholeheartedly and also thank God during any periods of silent prayer that occur before, during, or after worship. Cultivating thankful hearts will help us remember who God is and why He is worthy of our praise.

LIVING SACRIFICES IN WORSHIP

ROMANS 12:1 "I APPEAL TO YOU THEREFORE, BROTHERS, BY THE MERCIES OF GOD, TO PRESENT YOUR BODIES AS A LIV- ING SACRIFICE, HOLY AND ACCEPTABLE TO GOD, WHICH IS YOUR SPIRITUAL WORSHIP."

R ead through the Old Testament in even a cursory way and it is impossible to miss the place of animal sacrifices in old covenant worship. Much of the book of Leviticus, for example, consists of instructions for how to offer sacrifices properly. The Historical Books, the Psalms, and the Prophetic Books feature many references to the practice of sacrificing bulls, sheep, goats, and other creatures to the Lord.

Of course, sacrifices to atone for sin have ceased under the new covenant. Christ has fulfilled the purpose of the various sin offer- ings, so we do not offer up sacrifices to atone for sin any longer (Heb. 10:1–18). That does not mean, however, that we offer no sacrifices unto the Lord in the present era. As we see in today's passage, God's fundamental demand for our worship is that we offer ourselves to Him as a "living sacrifice" (Rom. 12:1).

Note the striking phrase "living sacrifice." Ordinarily, that which is sacrificed is dead. It has lost any say in its destiny because there is no life left within it. Something similar happens when we offer up ourselves to God as living sacrifices. Although we remain alive—indeed, we are more alive once we are in Christ than we were outside of Him—we are sacrifices unto God. We have sur- rendered any control we have over our life's mission and are now committed entirely to the lordship of another. By the Lord's irre- sistible grace, we have put ourselves in His hands and are His

III

DAY 49 & 50

to do with as He sees fit. Our Creator is not cruel or capricious, and we can be sure that He will never mistreat us. But He is our Master, and to be a Christian is to offer ourselves unreservedly for His use wherever He calls us. As Dr. R.C. Sproul writes in his commentary *Romans*, when we bow the knee to Christ Jesus, "we give ourselves to thank and serve Him." At root, our worship is our surrendering of ourselves to God Himself every day of our lives, and especially as we gather with God's people to praise His name.

Old covenant believers were called to offer the best of their animals, to offer up that which was without blemish (see Lev. 1:3). In our worship, we must do the same. We must not serve the Lord as a mere afterthought. We must not seek Him half-heartedly. Instead, we are to give Him the very best of ourselves, not to atone for our sin or to merit our forgiveness but to thank Him for saving us, for giving us a purpose, and for calling us into service.

FOR
FURTHER
STUDY
———
Psalm 4:5;
Ephesians
5:2;
Hebrews
13:10-16;
1 Peter
2:4-5

APPLICATION
Our spiritual worship consists of our offering ourselves to God as holy, acceptable living sacrifices. We pursue holiness because we want to offer to the Lord that which is pure. We seek to understand God's will for worship so that our praise is acceptable and offered according to His prescriptions. By the grace of God and for the sake of His glory, may we offer ourselves to Him unreservedly this day.

DAY 51

THE BEAUTY OF WORSHIP

PSALM 27:4 "ONE THING HAVE I ASKED OF THE Lord, THAT WILL I SEEK AFTER: THAT I MAY DWELL IN THE HOUSE OF THE Lord ALL THE DAYS OF MY LIFE, TO GAZE UPON THE BEAUTY OF THE Lord AND TO INQUIRE IN HIS TEMPLE."

 s we consider the various elements that Scripture reveals as essential parts of God-honoring worship, we find that they are enhanced by various art forms. The singing of prayers, psalms, and hymns involves the art of music. The places where we gather for worship are designed according to the art of architecture. We could give other examples, but the point is that the arts play a key role in worship. In order that we might have a biblical view of the fine arts, particularly regarding their role in worship, we will now spend a few days looking at what Scripture has to say about the arts. Dr. R.C. Sproul's teaching series *Recovering the Beauty of the Arts* will guide us.

When we study the Scriptures, it is very clear that our Creator is concerned with both goodness and truth. What we sometimes miss, however, is that our God likewise esteems beauty. In fact, the Bible—especially the Old Testament—contains many passages that praise the beauty of our Maker. Today's passage, for example, expresses David's desire to gaze upon "the beauty of the LORD" (Ps. 27:4).

Psalm 27 is particularly notable for its connection of worship with God's beauty. Since the old covenant saints did not see God face-to-face, the only way they could gaze upon the beauty of the Lord was to enter the tabernacle or temple and view the beauty of the structure and its furnishings. David notes his desire to dwell in the house of the Lord, which is a reference to the earthly sanctuary where God made His presence felt. The curtains, altar, lampstand, and other elements of the temple all revealed particular truths about the Lord. To see these things was, in a very limited sense, to gaze on the beauty of God.

We also see a connection of beauty and worship in the garments that the Old Testament priests wore. Exodus 28 relays the Lord's instructions for the priestly attire, which was to be made "for glory and for beauty" (v. 2). Obviously, the priests wore their priestly robes for service in the tabernacle and temple. God was not looking for something that was merely functional for worship in Israel; rather, He wanted the priests adorned in beautiful garments when they entered His presence.

The Lord was so concerned for beauty in old covenant worship that He employed skilled craftsmen in order to craft the tabernacle and its furnishings (31:1–11). God gifts artists in order to create beauty for His worship.

FOR FURTHER STUDY

Psalm 96:6; Mark 14:3-9

III

DAY 50 & 51

If God thought beauty was important for worship under the old covenant, how much more important is it for new covenant worship, since we have a clearer understanding of God's beauty through the life and ministry of Christ? Let us encourage our leaders to pursue beauty and excellence in worship, and may we seek to use our talents to help create such beauty if we are so gifted.

DAY 52

RITUAL VS. RITUALISM

JEREMIAH 7:1-4 "THUS SAYS THE Lord OF HOSTS, THE GOD OF ISRAEL: AMEND YOUR WAYS AND YOUR DEEDS, AND I WILL LET YOU DWELL IN THIS PLACE. DO NOT TRUST IN THESE DECEPTIVE WORDS: 'THIS IS THE TEMPLE OF THE Lord, THE TEMPLE OF THE Lord, THE TEMPLE OF THE Lord'" (VV. 3-4).

A s we consider the place of the arts in the Christian life and particularly in worship, we should note that coming out of the Reformation there were two broad approaches to the arts. Martin Luther, for example, was willing to preserve much of the art that had been present in the churches leading up to the Reformation. In fact, he returned from hiding in Wartburg Castle to put an end to the iconoclasm—the smashing of artwork in the churches—in which some of his radical followers were engaged. To this day, there continues to be much use of the visual arts in Lutheran worship.

In contrast, the Reformed tradition has been more hesitant to embrace the visual arts in worship. In Geneva, for example, John Calvin set out to simplify the liturgy and eliminate many of the visual elements present in church sanctuaries. Yet even Calvin was not opposed to the arts entirely. He believed that art still had a place in the Christian life, and he was willing to reintroduce music into the worship in Geneva once he had seen how valuable it was in Strasbourg's worship services.

Later in the Reformed tradition, the Puritans worked to purge what they saw as unbiblical intrusions into public worship. They sought to reform some of the liturgical practices of Anglicanism. While they wanted primarily to make Christian worship conform to what they believed was a simpler, more biblical pattern, we cannot overlook the concerns about ritualism that drove them. To this day, in fact, many Christians oppose elaborate liturgies because they believe they can produce people who simply go through the motions, who worship by rote without a heart commitment to Christ.

Scripture certainly warns us that our worship can become mere routine and that we can falsely put our trust in worship practices and elements and not in the Lord. In today's passage, for example, we read Jeremiah's warnings against the people of Judah who trusted in the fact that the temple stood in Jerusalem when they were confronted with their sin. They thought they could do whatever they wanted because they had the temple and the liturgy given by God. But they failed to understand that rituals are useless without faith (Jer. 7:1–4).

That is not to say that rituals are inherently bad. If they were, God could hardly have instituted the sacrificial system and other ritual events such as the Lord's Supper. The problem is not with rituals themselves but with ritualism, which happens when we go through the motions without an inner disposition to worship the Lord.

FOR FURTHER STUDY

1 Samuel 15:22-23; Amos 5:21-24; Matthew 23; 2 Timothy 3:1-5

APPLICATION

Any group of professing Christians can fall into ritualism. Even those with simpler liturgies can go through the motions without their hearts' truly being in the worship. It is a danger for all of us, so we should ask God to keep us devoted to Him, and we should seek to engage our entire being in worship every time we gather with God's people to praise our Creator.

III

DAY 51 & 52

FORMS AND THEIR COMMUNICATION

1 CORINTHIANS 14:40 "ALL THINGS SHOULD BE DONE
DECENTLY AND IN ORDER."

F ormalism or ritualism is always a threat to authentic worship. Throughout Scripture, for example, we find many warnings given to those who follow the prescribed worship practices with precision and yet do not bear the fruits of obedience to the moral law of God (Jer. 7:1–4; Matt. 23). At times, the Word of God even seems to suggest that given the choice between obedience to the moral law and following the prescribed rituals, you choose obedience to the moral law (1 Sam. 15:22–23; Amos 5:21–24). But such presentations are examples of hyperbole to help people pay attention to what they have been missing. Scripture's solution is actually to connect heart devotion and obedience to the prescribed practices. Ezekiel 36 and 40–48, for example, describe Israel's renewal as involving changed hearts and proper ritual practice even if those rituals are symbolic of the work of Christ. In other words, the prophets do not see the rituals themselves as inherently bad. The trouble is mere outward conformity to practices without an inner commitment to what the practices signify.

In an effort to avoid formalism and ritualism, some Christians have moved away from "high church" liturgies such as we might find in Anglicanism or Lutheranism in favor of "low church," less elaborate services often associated with independent or nondenominational worship. But even simpler orders of service are still liturgies. Even the Quakers, whose gatherings consist of sitting in silence until someone feels moved to speak, follow a liturgy—a plan for worship—because they have agreed to a system wherein they are quiet until "moved by the Spirit." And wherever you have a form or ritual, it is possible to go through the motions in a formalistic or ritualistic way. Our propensity for mere rote worship does not change simply by the altering of external forms, and we are all capable of putting on a show even when our hearts are not in what we are doing.

No matter the theological tradition from which we come, all worship involves art forms, and all forms communicate something. The form of a liturgy may communicate the belief that God desires simplicity or that He prizes complexity. A plainly decorated worship sanctuary may tell us that visual beauty is not especially prized by the Lord, while an elaborately decorated sanctuary may convey that God values visual beauty. The design of our buildings can communicate whether we see worship as having a kind of "entertainment value." Whatever form we use, we are sending a message.

APPLICATION

Though we may not always be conscious of it, all our forms communicate something. That is why it is important for our leaders to think carefully about what they do in worship and how they do it. It is also important for us to think about the forms we participate in as worshipers. Knowing what they communicate can help us be more knowledgeable worshipers.

FOR FURTHER STUDY

Numbers 4; Nehemiah 8; Matthew 6:5-6; John 4:24; 6:41-59

DAY 54

THE POWER OF MUSIC

1 SAMUEL 16:14-23 "WHENEVER THE HARMFUL SPIRIT FROM GOD WAS UPON SAUL, DAVID TOOK THE LYRE AND PLAYED IT WITH HIS HAND. SO SAUL WAS REFRESHED AND WAS WELL, AND THE HARMFUL SPIRIT DEPARTED FROM HIM" (V. 23).

M usic is a key component of most Christian worship services, and so it has also been at the center of many of the controversies that the church has faced regarding worship. Are instruments permitted in worship, or must we sing only a cappella? Should we stick to the classic hymns from the past, or may we use contemporary songs? These questions all concern music and the way we use it in our worship services.

Undoubtedly, the power of music explains why the battles over music and worship have been so fierce. So many of the most

III

DAY 53 & 54

important events of our lives have musical associations. Couples have "their song," which generally refers to a favored piece of music that has been particularly meaningful to their relationship. We might not remember the song we heard on the radio yesterday, but many of us remember a school alma mater or fight song because these tunes are connected to key memories from our youth.

The power of music is displayed in other ways as well. Music has been used on the battlefield to boost morale and give soldiers the emotional strength to fight. Entire worldviews are communicated in the songs of a particular generation. At least since Plato, older generations have lamented how the music of younger generations is corrupting youth morally and intellectually.

Scripture communicates the power and importance of music to us in many ways. The book of Psalms is filled with references to instruments and singing, indicating that music has an appropriate place in the worship of our Creator. In some cases, music also has a kind of spiritual power. Today's passage, for example, records the interesting account of David's ministry to King Saul through music. Evidently, the evil spirit that tormented Saul would flee whenever David, as court musician, took up his lyre and played for the king (1 Sam. 16:14–23).

FOR FURTHER STUDY
———
1 Chronicles 23:2-6; Zephaniah 3:17; Ephesians 5:18-21; Revelation 15:2-4

These examples of musical power indicate that we dare not be naive when we think about the kind of music we use in worship. Whatever music we use in worship, it will set a certain atmosphere, and it will either enhance the other elements of worship or create a sense of aesthetic and even theological dissonance. Its lyrics will either present God in all His majesty or obscure Him and His glory. Music is not a matter to be taken lightly. It is an art form, and all art forms communicate something to us.

APPLICATION

Scripture prescribes no particular kind of music, so the choices of music we use in worship and even for leisure must be guided by Christian wisdom. Is the music true, good, and beautiful? Does it present what is noble, pure, and praiseworthy? If our music does not do these things, it may not be appropriate for us to listen to in private and is certainly not appropriate for worship (Phil. 4:8).

MUSIC AND THEOLOGY

PSALM 101:1 "I WILL SING OF STEADFAST LOVE AND JUS-
TICE; TO YOU, O Lord, I WILL MAKE MUSIC."

N ot only was Martin Luther an accomplished theologian
and beloved pastor, but he also had some gifting for music.
He wrote many hymns, many of which are sung to this
day not only by those in the Lutheran tradition but by other Protestants as well. Perhaps the best known is "A Mighty Fortress Is
Our God," which is based on Psalm 46. Luther well understood
the power and influence of music. His understanding is well captured in his statement that "music is the handmaiden of theology."

Like a handmaiden who assists her master, music serves theology and the teaching of God's Word. And like a handmaiden,
music can be a good servant or a bad servant. When music is
a good servant, it provides the right setting for the teaching of
God's truth and for helping the people of God grasp the deep
things of the Lord. Quality hymns and songs enrich our hearts
and minds, driving home what God has revealed to His people.
On the other hand, when music is a bad servant, it gets in the way
of good theology. Poorly crafted music and lyrics promote error.
As an art form, music always communicates something, and it
can communicate either truth or error.

So many of the fights over music that occur in the church have
been over whether we should have contemporary hymns and
songs or stick to the classic music of the church. That debate can
obscure the real issues. After all, the classic hymns of the church
were contemporary music when they were first sung, and some
of the music written in our day will undoubtedly endure as classic
music for the people of God. No, the real debate is between good
music and mediocre or poor music. A beloved hymn is not necessarily a good hymn simply because it is old, for there are many
old hymns that teach poor theology. And a current song is not necessarily a bad song, for many current songs teach good theology.

At issue is whether a particular hymn or piece of music, in both

III

FOR
FURTHER
STUDY
—————
2 Samuel 6;
2 Chron-
icles 29;
Psalms
81:1-3;
92:1-4;
Colossians
3:16

the arrangement of notes and its lyrics, is able to convey biblical truth. Good worship music is able to convey something of the complexity of our Lord's character, and it invites us to increase our knowledge. Simplistic songs often do not do justice to the full biblical truth that they seek to express, and they often do not invite us to move deeper into God's Word to learn more and more about Him. Our goal should be to find the music that is best able to convey God's truth, goodness, and beauty.

APPLICATION

The biblical psalms model the kind of complexity that good sacred music has to offer. Psalm 101, for example, is an extended meditation on the love and justice of God as well as His wrath and our responsibility before the Lord. Pick one of the psalms today and meditate on what it says about our great God.

DAY 56

THE ARTS AND THE WORSHIP SPACE

2 CHRONICLES 5:1 "THUS ALL THE WORK THAT SOLOMON DID FOR THE HOUSE OF THE Lord WAS FINISHED. AND SOLOMON BROUGHT IN THE THINGS THAT DAVID HIS FATHER HAD DEDICATED, AND STORED THE SILVER, THE GOLD, AND ALL THE VESSELS IN THE TREASURIES OF THE HOUSE OF GOD."

E arly in Christian history, believers met for worship and for teaching in homes. We find evidence of this in the New Testament in places such as 1 Corinthians 16:19, where Paul shares greetings from "Aquila and Prisca, together with the church in their house." Later, during the Roman persecutions of the church, Christians would often meet for worship in the catacombs of Rome. Eventually, the growth of the church and the legalization of Christianity in the Roman Empire meant that more and more dedicated Christian sanctuaries were built. In the medieval period, Gothic cathedrals were routinely constructed throughout Europe. The Puritans favored plainer buildings, and today we can find new churches meeting in movie theaters or school auditoriums until they raise enough funds to build their own buildings.

Christians have worshiped in many different places and structures, and it is not hard to figure out why. After all, Jesus tells us in John 4:21–23 that there is not only one ordained place for new covenant worship. Moreover, the doctrine of God's omnipresence, taught in places such as Psalm 139:7, helps us understand that there are a wide variety of places where we can worship the Lord. If God is everywhere, then in the final analysis, we can worship Him anywhere.

It is interesting, however, that although God can be worshiped anywhere, believers have been almost invariably driven to build dedicated meeting spaces for worship when they have been able to do so. The notion of sacred space is hard to escape because we know that in worship we are entering into the very presence of God. We are, as it were, joining in heaven with the angels and with the saints who have gone before us to praise our Creator (Heb. 12:18–24). Christians have built worship sanctuaries to mark out a space separate from the world as an indication of that heavenly reality.

And since architecture is an art form, churches have been built to communicate truths about God. Lofty ceilings in Gothic cathedrals, for example, convey a sense of the transcendence of the Lord. Many churches have been built in the shape of the cross, for it is only in the shadow of our Savior's atoning death that we can have access to our Creator's presence. No matter how we build our sanctuaries, they will convey something about God to the people gathered there. May these buildings convey what is true, good, and beautiful.

FOR FURTHER STUDY

1 Kings 7:13-51; Romans 16:5

APPLICATION

Some professing Christians neglect public worship, saying that they can worship God anywhere, even while sitting on the beach. While it is true that God can be worshiped anywhere, we are not to neglect the corporate worship of God's people. No matter the kind of building your church worships in, do not neglect the weekly worship of God alongside your fellow believers.

III

DAY 55 & 56

IV

SANCTIFICATION

Sanctification is the term that the Bible uses to describe the process in which believers progressively become more like our Lord Jesus Christ. This process of sanctification begins when we are converted and continues until our death. While believers will never be fully sanctified in this life, we strive to love God and love others because our slavery to sin has been broken and our new hearts long to please our Lord and become more like Him.

Sanctification occurs as we behold the glory of the Lord and are empowered by the Holy Spirit to pursue Him more and more, becoming like Him as we do (2 Cor. 3:18). We are to expend effort in our sanctification, while at the same time understanding that God is the One who ultimately fuels our efforts (Phil. 2:12-13).

In this final section on the Christian life, we turn to this topic of sanctification, first looking at the life empowered by the Spirit and the use of spiritual gifts. We will then look at the topic of love in the life of the believer. And last, we explore the reality of discipline, trials, and suffering during this earthly sojourn, which will one day come to an end when we will behold God face-to-face in perfect joy for all eternity.

WALKING BY THE SPIRIT

GALATIANS 5:16-17 "BUT I SAY, WALK BY THE SPIRIT,
AND YOU WILL NOT GRATIFY THE DESIRES OF THE FLESH"
(V. 16).

S anctification, the process in which believers become progressively more like Jesus Christ, is a lifelong endeavor.
We are to strive for holiness while recognizing that the
power to do so comes from God Himself (Phil. 2:12–13). Consequently, we begin our look at sanctification by considering the
role of the Holy Spirit in our lives.

In seeking to walk according to God's commands, Christians
have always faced the problems of legalism and antinomianism.
Legalism tries to thwart sin and promote holiness through impos-
ing a law code that adds to Scripture. Of course, Paul addresses
legalism in Galatians due to the false teachers who wanted to
circumcise gentile believers even though God never says that gentile disciples of Christ must become Jews (proselytes, Gal. 5:2–6).

Those who embrace antinomianism misinterpret Christian
liberty, seeking to eliminate standards entirely. Antinomians
indulge their flesh, which refers to human nature in rebellion
against the Lord (Rom. 8:8). Legalism is a common response to
antinomianism, and Paul defines the true way not to indulge the
flesh in today's passage, answering the Galatian Judaizers who
bolstered their appeal to the law by saying that keeping it is the
only way to avoid sin.

Most legalists try to be faithful to God's call to be holy (Lev.
11:44), but their good intentions do not produce right results. For
as Paul tells us, the only way to keep from gratifying the desires
of the flesh is to "walk by the Spirit" (Gal. 5:16). The basic idea
here is that the Christian life is one defined by the fruit of the
Spirit, which fulfills the law (vv. 22–23). We are to be constantly
dependent on the Spirit for living in a manner pleasing to God.
Again, a life under the law is not a life without any directives.
Paul talks about the Spirit-led life and fulfilling the law through

love in the same context (vv. 13–15), indicating that to walk by the Spirit produces a manner of life characterized by love for God and neighbor, the two great commandments (Matt. 22:34–40).

Living in the Spirit is incompatible with living in the flesh— with being dominated by sin—since the flesh and the Spirit are at odds with one another (Gal. 5:17). It is not a life free from all sin, for we will fall into transgression on occasion until death (1 John 1:8–9). But it is a life in which evil does not reign because the Holy Spirit Himself compels us to follow God's will (Jer. 31:31–34). We who walk by the Spirit uphold the law, not in our own power but in putting to death any idea that we can keep our Creator's law in our own strength and drawing upon the Spirit's might to make us please the Lord (Eph. 5:18).

FOR FURTHER STUDY

Deuteronomy 23:14; Isaiah 44:1-5; John 6:63; 1 John 1:5-7

APPLICATION

John Calvin comments, "If we would obey the Spirit, we must labor, and fight, and apply our utmost energy; and we must begin with self-denial." Walking by the Holy Spirit is the denial of the self and one's fleshly desires and turning to Christ to follow His example, asking the Spirit to enable us to do so. Consider today where you might be following the desires of the flesh and not the way of the Spirit. Repent and ask the Spirit to help you follow Jesus.

DAY 58

NOT UNDER THE LAW

GALATIANS 5:18 "BUT IF YOU ARE LED BY THE SPIRIT, YOU ARE NOT UNDER THE LAW."

P aul's admonition that we walk in the Spirit so as not to gratify the flesh (Gal. 5:16) points to the believer's ongoing struggle. Already we enjoy salvation, having received the Spirit through faith in Jesus (Eph. 1:13–14). Still, our fleshly nature is not yet obliterated even though our glorification is sure (Rom. 8:1–30). Until death, our evil desires oppose the Spirit (Gal. 5:17), the war growing more heated as the Spirit reveals our sin

IV

DAY 57 & 58

to us, conforming us to Christ. Martin Luther says, "The more godly a man is, the more does he feel that battle."

Following the Holy Spirit's lead, we mortify the flesh (v. 16; see Rom. 8:13) and are not "under the law" (Gal. 5:18). Certainly, not being under Torah cannot mean that its ethics are now optional. Otherwise, God denies His own standards, which is impossible (Rom. 7:12; 2 Tim. 2:13). Moreover, Galatians 5:18 in context shows that those not led by the Spirit break the so-called moral laws of the old covenant. The Mosaic law forbids sexual immorality, idolatry (Ex. 20:3, 14), and all the other works of the flesh in Galatians 5:19–21. But to bear the Spirit's fruit is to fulfill the law, for love is commanded therein (Gal. 5:22; see Lev. 19:18). Even though we are not "under the law," by the Spirit we live it out.

If those in the flesh and those under the law are not Spirit-led (Gal. 5:16, 18), then to be under the law is to be in the flesh. To be under the law is to repeat the error of the Israelites who in bondage to sin looked to the Mosaic law as an end in itself, not as a guardian to take them to the Messiah (Rom. 6:14–23; Gal. 3:21–26). As Augustine says, people "under the law" are motivated by the law's threatened torments, not love of righteousness. They do the law outwardly to avoid punishment, not from the heart, the font of impurity (Matt. 5:21–30; 15:18–20). Therefore, they do not see the depth of their iniquity or need of grace.

Yet we are led by the Spirit and know that we cannot keep the law in our own power. We see Torah not as an end in itself, as if we ourselves can through its statutes kill the flesh; rather, seeing our sin defined in the law, we daily turn to Jesus for pardon, drawing upon the Spirit to crush evil (Rom. 8:5, 13).

FOR FURTHER STUDY

Micah 3:8; Mark 4:1-20; Galatians 5:25; Jude 20-21

APPLICATION

John Calvin says that not being under law means that we are "free from the dominion of the law, which will act only in the capacity of a kind adviser, and will no longer lay a restraint upon [our] consciences." As Christians, we are not bound to sin any longer but free to serve God joyfully and truly love our neighbors as ourselves. Ask the Lord to empower you to walk in that freedom and serve Him in the Spirit today by doing a good deed for a neighbor.

DAY 59

THE WORKS OF THE FLESH

GALATIANS 5:19-21 "I WARN YOU, AS I WARNED YOU
BEFORE, THAT THOSE WHO DO SUCH THINGS WILL NOT
INHERIT THE KINGDOM OF GOD" (V. 21).

C hristian freedom cannot be understood without distinguishing it from modern ideas of liberty. Many people define freedom as the ability to do whatever we desire without fear of consequences. But this is false liberty, for the more we indulge our sinful desires, the more binding our evil inclinations become (Rom. 1:18–32). Biblical freedom, however, is liberty from our fleshly nature and the ability to follow the Spirit into holiness (Gal. 5:13–18).

Withdrawal from the world into a life defined by the Mosaic law, not our union with Christ, is not the answer to evil. Old covenant Israel's failure to keep the Torah and glad embrace of pagan ways reveals that submission to grace and the pursuit of God's Spirit is the only way to defeat sin (Isa. 32:14–17; Rom. 9:30–10:4), since life in the Holy Spirit is incompatible with the works of the flesh.

Paul lists such works in Galatians 5:19–21 as he continues to exposit Christian freedom, demonstrating that real liberty is not licentiousness. His list is not exhaustive, and he gives only a representative sample of wicked deeds (v. 21). Also, the works of the flesh are condemned in the so-called moral portions of the Law (see Ex. 20:1–17); thus, even though we are not related to the Torah in the same way as were old covenant believers, we are still to live according to its ethical emphases. Some works of the flesh, like envy, tend to be inward in nature and invisible to others. This warns us to examine our hearts daily that we might kill the flesh both inwardly and outwardly. Moreover, dissensions and rivalries are often nurtured within the church itself. Let us not call holy a divisive spirit that invites us to break fellowship over trivial matters.

The works of the flesh are contrary to life in the Spirit (Gal.

IV

DAY 58 & 59

5:21), and all who do them habitually and unrepentantly prove that they never received the Spirit and never had real faith. Those led by the Holy Spirit prove it not by never doing such works but in repenting of them and striving against them (1 John 1:5–10). Martin Luther writes, "It is one thing to be provoked by the flesh, and another thing to assent to the flesh, and without fear or remorse to perform and fulfill the works thereof, and to continue therein, and yet to counterfeit holiness."

APPLICATION

FOR
FURTHER
STUDY

Leviti-
cus 18;
Colossians
3:5-11

Take the time today to do a "spiritual inventory" and consider whether any of the works of the flesh in Galatians 5:19–21 are characteristic of your life. If you have a trusted Christian friend, ask him or her if any of these things are true about you. If so, repent and turn away from these works. Run to the grace of Christ, who will forgive all those who follow Him. If these works are not characteristic of you, stand guard in the power of the Spirit, lest you fall into them.

DAY 60

THE FRUIT OF THE SPIRIT

GALATIANS 5:22-23 "THE FRUIT OF THE SPIRIT IS LOVE, JOY, PEACE, PATIENCE, KINDNESS, GOODNESS, FAITHFULNESS, GENTLENESS, SELF-CONTROL; AGAINST SUCH THINGS THERE IS NO LAW."

I f, as Paul writes, Christian freedom is not licentiousness or legalism (Gal. 5:16–21), what does it mean to "walk by the Spirit"? The answer, the Apostle demonstrates, is seen in our manifestation of the Spirit's fruit (vv. 22–24).

Let us begin with two observations about Paul's use of the fruit metaphor itself. First, there is a degree of inevitability with the word *fruit*—well-nourished apple trees inevitably produce apples. Likewise, believers, as those who abide in Christ through the Holy Spirit, cannot help but yield lives in which the Spirit's fruit predominates, not evil works (John 15:1–11; Gal. 5:19–21). In so doing, they fulfill the vocation given to Israel (Isa. 5:1–4). Second, the Greek word *karpos* or "fruit" in Galatians 5:22 is singular. Paul lists many different virtues in verses 22–23, but there is a unity to them. The "fruits" of the Spirit are one; thus, none of them is optional. John Calvin comments that only those who bear all the fruit, to one degree or another, prove themselves to be in Christ.

We see evidence for the unity of the fruit in that Paul places love, the only quality to appear in all the other New Testament listings of spiritual traits (see 1 Cor. 13:13; 1 Tim. 4:12; 2 Peter 1:5–7), at the top of his list (Gal. 5:22). Commentators both ancient and modern agree that love is the root of all of the fruits in Galatians 5:22–23; in fact, they are manifestations of love, the chief Christian virtue, the one that will last forever (1 Cor. 13:8). The church father Jerome remarks: "Without love other virtues are not reckoned to be virtues. From love is born all that is good." God is love (1 John 4:8), and to imitate Him as we walk by the Spirit is to love others.

Paul expands upon these other fruits in the rest of the book of Galatians. For today's reading, note that the Apostle includes joy in his list (Gal. 5:22). Martin Luther writes that this proves that God "hates comfortless doctrine, heavy and sorrowful cogitations, and loves cheerful hearts." Theology must always end in doxology—the joyful praise of our Creator; otherwise, we have not truly studied the things of God.

FOR FURTHER STUDY

2 Chronicles 5:13; Song of Solomon 8:6-7; Hosea 11:4; Hebrews 13:1

APPLICATION

The love commended in Galatians 5:22–23 is also the greatest apologetic for the Christian faith (John 13:35) and is defined by the character of God, who loves us both when He commends our obedience and when He condemns our sin, calling us to repentance. Like Him, we are to love those who are difficult to love. This week, strive to show love for another person in word and deed, particularly if that person is often "unlovable."

IV

DAY 59 & 60

LIVING BY THE SPIRIT

GALATIANS 5:24-26 "IF WE LIVE BY THE SPIRIT, LET
US ALSO KEEP IN STEP WITH THE SPIRIT. LET US NOT
BECOME CONCEITED, PROVOKING ONE ANOTHER, ENVYING ONE
ANOTHER" (VV. 25-26).

G alatians 5:19–21 is not an exhaustive listing of the works
of the flesh, and verses 22–23 are likewise selective. Passages like 2 Peter 1:5–7 give spiritual fruits not found in Galatians; thus, we need to study all of Scripture in order to get a full record of the traits that define those who live by the Spirit.

Those who have crucified the flesh (the remnant of opposition to God within) walk in the Spirit and bear His fruit. In fact, all who belong to Christ Jesus have crucified the flesh, Paul reminds us (Gal. 5:24), but the Greek verb here tells us that this crucifixion is both a past event and a lifelong effort. James Montgomery Boice's comments on Galatians in *The Expositor's Bible Commentary* illustrate how this can be the case. True, Jesus defeated evil at Calvary, ending sin and death's dominion. Yet just as a man nailed to a tree can live for days, gasping for breath despite being as good as dead, so too can our lingering sin rear its ugly head at times. On these occasions we must nail the flesh back to the cross, as it were, refusing to yield to temptation. Martin Luther writes, "The faithful . . . so long as they live here crucify the flesh; that is to say, they feel the lusts thereof, but they obey them not."

Luther adds that walking according to the Spirit is being armed with God's Word, faith, prayer, and the sacraments that we might not yield to the flesh. Moreover, cultivating a humble attitude is also essential to walking by the Spirit, as today's passage indicates (vv. 25–26). Meekness and humility—not viewing oneself more highly than one ought and the refusal to boast in one's own abilities or be envious of others—has always marked those in whom the Spirit dwells (Num. 12:3, 7). Furthermore, these characteristics remain among those that the world finds least desirable. Politicians are too proud to admit their mistakes, philanthropists boast in their generosity, but Christians must exemplify humility, not envying others and repenting toward the Almighty and one another when they sin. Indeed, a life of repentance and faith evidences the leading of the Holy Spirit, for those who are humble before the Lord are those to whom He gives the grace of salvation (1 Peter 5:5) and, consequently, the gift of His Spirit (Gal. 3:2).

FOR FURTHER STUDY

Proverbs 18:12; Isaiah 66:1-2; Matthew 5:5; 18:1-4; James 1:21

APPLICATION

Luther offers the following application: God is no respecter of persons, and since all believers serve Him by the same faith with the same Spirit, the layman who faithfully uses the gift that the Lord has given him pleases God no less than the minister. "Wherefore we ought to regard the lowliest Christians no less than they regard us." None of us should boast in our calling or think that we are either better or worse off than others because of our particular gifts.

DAY 62

USING OUR GIFTS

ROMANS 12:6-8 "HAVING GIFTS THAT DIFFER ACCORDING TO THE GRACE GIVEN TO US, LET US USE THEM" (V. 6A).

W e as Christians experience a definitive transformation in our conversion when the Holy Spirit releases us from our bondage to sin and brings us out of darkness into the marvelous light of God (1 Peter 2:9–10). Yet the Spirit of God does not stop there. He continues His work of transformation throughout our lives, bringing us more and more into conformity to the image of Christ through the renewing of our minds according to His Word (Rom. 12:1–2). This is the Christian doctrine of sanctification, that aspect of our salvation wherein we cooperate with our Creator to put our remaining sin to death and to develop affections and actions that are pleasing to Him. Other aspects of our salvation such as regeneration and justification are not cooperative. The Holy Spirit alone changes our hearts, and

IV

DAY 61 & 62

103

only the righteousness of Christ secures for us the declaration that we are righteous before God. But we cooperate with the Lord in sanctification as we "work out [our] own salvation with fear and trembling," though even here God takes the initiative and undergirds all our efforts. We work out our salvation only because the Lord effectually works in us "both to will and to work for his good pleasure" (Phil. 2:12–13).

God the Holy Spirit animates us for sanctification through the preaching of His Word; therefore, the Apostles give us so many admonitions for our Christian growth. Having said that each of us is a member of the body of Christ and possesses a specific function (Rom. 12:3–5), Paul exhorts us in today's passage to use our gifts and fulfill our roles in the church. His list of gifts is not a comprehensive catalog of all the spiritual gifts that the Lord grants to His people, and it is one of several lists found in the New Testament. In any case, let us note that the Apostle assumes that all believers have at least one of the spiritual gifts mentioned in Scripture. This fact reveals an aspect of the new covenant's superiority over the old covenant. In the old covenant, ministerial gifts were limited mostly to the prophets, priests, and kings, but every believer is gifted in some way under the new covenant administration.

FOR
FURTHER
STUDY

Psalm
76:11-12;
Ezekiel
20:40;
1 Timo-
thy 4:14;
2 Timothy
1:6

Paul's overriding theme in Romans 12:6–8 is that we are not to exercise our spiritual gifts half-heartedly, but we must diligently and enthusiastically serve God and His people with our gifts. We do not all have the same gifts, but we have all received the same grace in Christ. According to this grace, the Spirit gifts us as He wills. We must not envy those who have different gifts than we do; rather, we must use the gifts we have to bless other people.

APPLICATION

Some people do not use their spiritual gifts because they do not know what they are. Others do not feel the freedom to use their gifts because their local church lacks an atmosphere that encourages the laity to do ministry. Those of us who are church leaders and teachers should develop a church culture that provides opportunities for many different kinds of service. And we are all responsible, with the help of other Christians, to discern the gifts that God has given us.

GENUINE GOODNESS AND LOVE

ROMANS 12:9 "LET LOVE BE GENUINE. ABHOR WHAT IS EVIL; HOLD FAST TO WHAT IS GOOD."

S cripture tells us that "God is love" (1 John 4:7–8). Of course, there is a great deal of confusion in our day as to what love means, so there are all manner of false understandings of the love of God both in the church and the world. A true understanding of divine love must take into account all of the Lord's other attributes, including His holiness and justice. In His love, God does not overlook sin, and we are constrained by His love to be holy as He is holy (1 Peter 1:8, 13–21). A true understanding of God's love will not compromise His holiness for the sake of a love that makes no demands of the beloved.

Because love is one of God's attributes, any understanding of what it means to be made in His image and to live in a way that pleases Him must take love into account. After all, though we are fallen, we still bear the image of our Creator, and we are being transformed into the image of Christ, who is Himself the perfect image of God (Gen. 1:26–27; 2 Cor. 3:18; Col. 1:15). We find it no surprise, therefore, that Paul includes a discussion of love in his description of what the life of people being transformed by God's Spirit looks like.

Romans 12:9a tells us that our love must "be genuine." This idea seems simple enough, and we can hardly do better than Dr. R.C. Sproul's comments on verse 9a in his commentary *Romans*: "God expects from us authentic love, that which is not mixed with hypocrisy or false sentiment." Genuine love does not make a show of affection that is not rooted in the realities of the heart. While it is good to treat people kindly and to love them in such a way that we go the extra mile for them, we have not truly pleased the

IV

DAY 62 & 63

Lord with such actions if we harbor hatred in our heart for them all the while we do such things (Matt. 5:21–26, 38–48).

Importantly, today's passage seems to serve as a section heading for what follows in the rest of Romans 12. In other words, the admonitions in verses 9b–21 define what genuine love means. Understanding what the Apostle teaches in these verses will help us know what true love looks like and keep us from succumbing to the false ideas of love present in our own culture. Verse 9b indicates that we are to "abhor what is evil; hold fast to what is good." We see here that love does not lead us to do what is wrong. Many people justify all sorts of illicit relationships in the name of love. But even if we "feel" like we are in love or "feel" like we are showing love, we do not experience godly love if we engage in something that God forbids in His law.

FOR
FURTHER
STUDY

1 Corin-
thians 13;
1 John
4:11

APPLICATION

Today we see a false understanding of love manifested most commonly in romantic relationships. Many people justify adultery by saying that they no longer love their spouse but love another person. People often justify homosexual relationships by saying, "As long as two people love each other, their genders do not matter." But God says that adultery, homosexual partnerships, and many other relationships are evil, and those engaging in them are not practicing true love.

DAY 64

LOVING AFFECTION AND HONOR

ROMANS 12:10-11 "LOVE ONE ANOTHER WITH BROTHERLY AFFECTION. OUTDO ONE ANOTHER IN SHOWING HONOR. DO NOT BE SLOTHFUL IN ZEAL, BE FERVENT IN SPIRIT, SERVE THE LORD."

 ove is the supreme Christian virtue (1 Cor. 13:13), but not everything that people call "love" is love in the biblical sense. To love as God demands, we must understand what

His infallible revelation tells us about genuine, holy love, and we find a description of this love in Romans 12:9–21. As we saw in our last devotional, love abhors what is evil (v. 9b). No relationship or affection that embraces what the Lord forbids fits the definition of true, God-honoring love. Instead, godly love clings only to what is good. Love seeks out, thinks on, and develops an affection for those things that are true, honorable, just, pure, lovely, commendable, excellent, and praiseworthy according to the Word of God (Phil. 4:8).

On the human-to-human level, John tells us that we must see the love that God demands first and foremost in the church itself (1 John 4:7–8). Thus, it makes sense for the Apostle Paul to focus first on what godly love looks like in the context of our relationships with other believers. We are first to "love one another with brotherly affection" (Rom. 12:10a). Paul wants us to consider other believers as our family, to show the same kind of undying love that binds brothers and sisters together. In fact, fellow Christians are more truly related to us as family members than are our flesh-and-blood relatives who are not believers.

This affection outdoes "one another in showing honor" (v. 10b). We are to be eager to recognize and applaud the achievements and service of others. When we show deference to others and praise them genuinely and quickly, we are showing forth the kind of humility that does not regard ourselves more highly than we ought, and therefore does not fail in its desire to see others properly commended for what they have done (v. 3).

Romans 12:11 emphasizes how godly love works itself out in how we relate to and serve our Creator. First, we read the needed admonition that we should "not be slothful in zeal." As part of our sinful condition, we often tend to start out on a new path with excitement but then grow weary in doing well. We must not do this in regard to our relationship with the Lord, and the Apostle's exhortation is one that we all need to hear.

Of course, we cannot work up or sustain love and zeal for the Lord by our own efforts, but we must continually rely on the work of His Holy Spirit in our own spirits. That is what the Apostle means when he calls us to "be fervent in spirit" (v. 11).

FOR
FURTHER
STUDY

We must daily call upon the Spirit to create in us a zeal for the things of God.

Deuteronomy
15:7-11;
2 Sam-
uel 9;
Acts 18:24-
28; 1 John
3:11-24

APPLICATION

Zeal for the Lord does not mean uncontrolled exuberance or a passion that is not in submission to what God has told us. We see this in Paul's admonition that our zeal must "serve the Lord" (Rom. 12:11). We cannot serve the Lord if we do not know what the Lord demands, so we must continually return to His Word. God's Holy Spirit does not work apart from the Word He inspired, and zeal that transgresses His revelation is not godly zeal.

DAY 65

HOPE AND HOSPITALITY

ROMANS 12:12-13 "REJOICE IN HOPE, BE PATIENT IN TRIBULATION, BE CONSTANT IN PRAYER. CONTRIBUTE TO THE NEEDS OF THE SAINTS AND SEEK TO SHOW HOSPITALITY."

G od's saving grace is effectual—it always accomplishes the salvation of those to whom it is given. The Lord cannot fail to finish the good work that He begins in us (Phil. 1:6–7). He will transform us into men and women who bear His image in perfect holiness.

Of course, we cannot achieve perfect holiness in this life; as long as sin abides, we always fall short of the Lord's demands in some way (1 John 1:8–10). So we cannot find our justification in our own good works or even the change that the Spirit works in us. Only Christ's perfect righteousness, imputed to us through faith in Him alone, can avail before the judgment seat of God and guarantee our heavenly citizenship (2 Cor. 5:21; Gal. 2:15–16). But justification never occurs without sanctification following on its heels (James 2:14–26). Those whom the Lord justifies are also granted His Spirit, and as we walk by this Spirit, we begin to fulfill our Creator's charge to love one another and to serve Him with zeal (Rom. 12:1–11).

As we love God and others more and more, we gain further assurance of our secure hope that this love will be perfected, that one day we will fully love the Lord our God with all that we are, and that we will love our neighbors as we love ourselves (Matt. 22:34–40; 1 John 4:7–21). This hope gives us cause to rejoice, as the Apostle Paul indicates in today's passage (Rom. 12:12). Yet as we see more clearly and rejoice more completely in the hope that God will complete the work of salvation that He has begun in us, we also understand that trials and tribulations litter the road to our final possession of this hope. Scripture clearly teaches that suffering is the lot of those who follow Christ (Acts 14:19–23). Thus, Paul also calls us to endurance in the midst of these difficulties, and following upon that, he exhorts us to constancy in prayer (Rom. 12:12). Left to ourselves, we cannot endure the pain that attends serving Christ in this fallen world, but through prayerful dependence on Him while we suffer, we are perfected over the course of our lives (James 1:2–4).

Those who love the Lord genuinely, who long for the day when their hope will be realized and their love will lack nothing, will love their brothers and sisters in tangible ways. Paul makes this point in Romans 12:13 with his exhortation "Contribute to the needs of the saints and seek to show hospitality." The sense in the Greek is that we are to go out of our way to provide for fellow believers who lack the basic necessities to sustain life and that we are to welcome Christians into our homes when they are traveling or otherwise in need.

FOR FURTHER STUDY

Genesis 18:1-8;
Proverbs 14:31;
Hebrews 13:2;
3 John 5-8

APPLICATION

Because there were not many inns in the ancient world, hospitality was particularly necessary. That need continues today, even in countries where hotels and other lodging options are abundant. We should seek to show hospitality whenever we can, whether by providing a meal for someone in our church, welcoming missionaries, or meeting other needs. In so doing, we love our brothers and sisters in Christ, and the love of God is fulfilled in us.

IV

DAY 64 & 65

REJOICING WITH OTHERS

ROMANS 12:14-15 "BLESS THOSE WHO PERSECUTE YOU; BLESS AND DO NOT CURSE THEM. REJOICE WITH THOSE WHO REJOICE, WEEP WITH THOSE WHO WEEP."

W ith the enablement of God's Spirit, living as a faithful disciple of Christ is possible (Phil. 2:12–13)—but it is certainly not easy. Christ's command for us to take up our cross indicates that following Him is difficult (Mark 8:34–35), but that is not all He has to say about the arduous nature of discipleship. Recall, for example, our Savior's admonition to love our enemies, a command that Paul echoes in today's passage (Matt. 5:43–48; Rom. 12:14).

Proverbs 25:21–22 encourages us not to treat our enemies the way that they treat us, but first-century Jews were not known for blessing their enemies. The idea was even stranger for the pagan Romans, who, unlike the Jews, did not have the benefit of possessing God's Word. The admonition is no easier for us today, considering our instinctive response to those who mistreat us. We find it almost impossible to put this teaching to love our enemies into practice. It takes a special, divine kind of love to bless one's enemies, and our Savior Himself makes this most evident, loving us enough to bless us by dying for us when we were yet God-hating sinners (Rom. 5:8). God gives us a divine kind of love when He changes us, and when we walk in it by the power of His Spirit, we can indeed bless our enemies. Such blessing is not mere endurance but actually wishes our foes well in our thoughts and actions.

Blessing our enemies, however, does not mean that we may never call for judgment upon them at the proper time. After all, Paul anathematized those who persecute the true church of God by twisting the gospel (Gal. 1:8–9; 6:12). Moreover, many imprecatory psalms in the Old Testament call on the Lord to destroy the enemies of Israel, and even Jesus Himself declared woes upon the Pharisees (Matt. 23). Apparently, calling for our Creator to judge our enemies is not inappropriate in cases of grave, impenitent assaults on His church. We reconcile this with God's call to bless our foes by holding out hope that the Lord will judge our enemies as He has judged us—namely, by crushing our sin on the cross and changing us into His friends. On this side of heaven, any call for judgment must embrace the hope that God would bring salvation to our enemies through judgment as He has done for us.

Sincere love for our enemies manifests itself in our blessing them. True affection is on display in the Christian community when we "rejoice with those who rejoice" and "weep with those who weep." In the church, there must be no envy over others' success, and we must enter into the grief of other suffering believers.

FOR FURTHER STUDY

Exodus 20:17; Proverbs 14:30; 1 Corinthians 4:12; Galatians 5:26

APPLICATION

Dr. R.C. Sproul writes in his commentary *Romans*, "There are no politics of envy in the kingdom of God." It is unnatural for our sinful flesh to rejoice when others receive blessings that we do not receive or when they succeed where we fail. That is why we must cultivate a joyful attitude that celebrates when others succeed and receive the things that we most want for ourselves. Only the Holy Spirit can enable us to do this, and He will do so as we call upon His assistance.

DAY 67

HARMONIOUS LIVING

ROMANS 12:16-17 "LIVE IN HARMONY WITH ONE ANOTHER. DO NOT BE HAUGHTY, BUT ASSOCIATE WITH THE LOWLY. NEVER BE WISE IN YOUR OWN SIGHT. REPAY NO ONE EVIL FOR EVIL, BUT GIVE THOUGHT TO DO WHAT IS HONORABLE IN THE SIGHT OF ALL."

IV

E nvy comes naturally to fallen humanity. Early on in the Bible, we see this clearly. Cain's envy over Abel's approval before God motivated him to commit the very first murder (Gen. 4:1–8). Yet even when it does not lead to murder, envy

DAY 66 & 67

exercises a powerful influence throughout society and even in the church itself. We dare not tolerate envy in our hearts, for it destroys the love that desires for others the good we want for ourselves. Instead, we must rejoice when others rejoice and weep when others weep (Rom. 12:15).

We will find this to be an impossible task as long as we are of different minds in the church. Paul's admonition for us to "live in harmony with one another" in Romans 12:16a calls all believers to have the same mindset regarding what the Lord requires of His people in terms of Christian conduct. This is a call not for us to have identical opinions on every matter but for us to strive for unity in the truth amid the diversity of personalities and gifts in the church. We are to seek to get along, to find unity in the truth of the gospel, not going to war over every small matter that may divide us. In sum, as Dr. R.C. Sproul writes in his commentary *Romans*, God "wants us to be people who do not love a fight."

A prideful spirit that is unwilling to admit when one is wrong and that makes one's own knowledge and wisdom the inflexible standard for what is wise will impede such unity every time. How can we grow in unity and harmony if we believe that we cannot be corrected or that it is beneath us to associate ourselves with those people whom the world considers lowly and insignificant? Thus, we find Paul condemning pride in verse 16b so that we might cast aside all stumbling blocks to unity in the body of Christ.

The Apostle shifts focus in verse 17 to explain what genuine love looks like in the context of the Christian's relationship to non-Christian society. After telling us not to repay evil for evil, which reminds us that our first instinct should be to bless others, not to curse them, Paul exhorts us to "give thought to do what is honorable in the sight of all." We dare not base our ethics on the standards of nonbelievers, but we must remember that because they bear God's image, they never suppress entirely the consciences they possess (Rom. 1:18–32; 2:14–16). Non-Christians do not have transformed hearts and cannot do what is fully pleasing to God. But they can—albeit imperfectly—recognize goodness, and we bring reproach on the name of Christ when we do not live up to the good that the pagans rightly discern.

FOR FURTHER STUDY

2 Chronicles 9:1-10; Daniel 6; 1 Corinthians 5; 1 Timothy 3:7

APPLICATION

The world does not always understand what is good, and sometimes it even calls "good" what is evil and "evil" what is good. Still, unbelievers often recognize what is right and true, and they definitely know when we do not practice what we preach. We cannot control the world's opinion of us, but we can control how consistently we live up to what we say. So that we do not bring reproach on the name of Christ, may we all "practice what we preach" and be quick to repent when we do not.

DAY 68

PEACEABLE LIVING

ROMANS 12:18 "IF POSSIBLE, SO FAR AS IT DEPENDS ON YOU, LIVE PEACEABLY WITH ALL."

L oving others genuinely according to Paul's command in Romans 12:9 requires a new heart that only God can give us by the regenerating power of His Holy Spirit through the preaching of His Word (Ezek. 36:26–27; 1 Peter 1:22–25). Therefore, the exhortations we find in Scripture to love people inside the church and in the larger society are not commands that our Creator expects us to fulfill in our own power. Instead, since they are His own words given by His own Spirit (2 Tim. 3:16–17), these commands and standards carry with them divine power that enables us to do what God tells us to do.

Because Scripture is the Word of God, it always presents the true and fully realistic view of God's creation. We see a great example of this in today's passage when Paul tells us, "If possible, so far as it depends on you, live peaceably with all" (Rom. 12:18). In this verse we find a recognition that getting along with some people in this world is often difficult—if not impossible. The Apostle understands that our relationships with others are two-way streets. There is only so much that we can do. We cannot change the hearts of other individuals. We cannot force them to like us or give us the benefit of the doubt. Some people will still

IV

DAY 67 & 68

hate us even if we bend over backward to show them kindness and mercy. Despite our best efforts, there will be people who will oppose us even when we go the extra mile for them.

That reality, Paul says, should not keep us from striving for peace with others in this world; rather, we must be peacemakers and live harmoniously with others as long as we do not compromise God's truth to do so. Still, there is only so much we can do—"So far as it depends on [us]." The Lord calls us only to do what is ours to do—namely, to apologize when we offend people unnecessarily, to seek the well-being even of our enemies, and to make sure that we do not put up a stumbling block to living at peace with others. If we do such things, we should be confident that we have done what our Creator requires. We cannot force others to be at peace with us, and the Lord does not expect us to do His work of softening the hearts of others toward us. Our task is to give no one a legitimate reason to be at war with us. If people are at war with us only because we are standing for the gospel, we have fulfilled this admonition. If they fight with us because we are obnoxious, cantankerous, or mean-spirited, or for any similar reason, we have not obeyed Paul's admonition.

FOR FURTHER STUDY

Jeremiah 29:7; 1 Thessalonians 5:13b

APPLICATION

Christ calls us to do whatever we can to live at peace with all people. This does not mean denying the truth; rather, it means cultivating a gentle spirit that seeks the good of all, that is humble enough to confess one's faults and failures, and that puts the needs of others before our own. Only as we walk in the Spirit will we do this. May we seek to be peacemakers and to do whatever we can to commend the name of Christ by living at peace with others insofar as it depends upon us.

DAY 69

LEAVING VENGEANCE TO THE LORD

ROMANS 12:19-20 "BELOVED, NEVER AVENGE YOURSELVES, BUT LEAVE IT TO THE WRATH OF GOD, FOR IT IS WRITTEN,

'VENGEANCE IS MINE, I WILL REPAY, SAYS THE LORD.'
TO THE CONTRARY, 'IF YOUR ENEMY IS HUNGRY, FEED
HIM; IF HE IS THIRSTY, GIVE HIM SOMETHING TO DRINK;
FOR BY SO DOING YOU WILL HEAP BURNING COALS ON HIS
HEAD.' "

A s we have seen, God does not call us to do what we cannot do and change the hearts of people so that they will be receptive to us, so as to constrain them to live at peace with us. Our only job is to live peaceably with all people as much as it depends upon us—all we are called to do is not give people a legitimate reason to be at war with us because we are rude, uncaring, or otherwise living in the flesh (Rom. 12:18).

This practical principle recognizes that at times there will be nothing we can do to have a harmonious relationship with others, for there are some individuals who will not like us no matter how we act. In today's passage, the Apostle Paul expands upon this principle with a look at our responsibilities when we encounter people who not only dislike us but also actively seek to inflict harm upon us. When people actively work evil against us, we are not to avenge ourselves. On the contrary, God calls us to trust Him to set things right, to give people what they deserve for standing against us (v. 19).

We all find this admonition difficult to follow, but we may have an easier time of it when we remember the perfect justice of our Creator (Deut. 32:4). It is better to trust God to avenge us, for His vengeance is pure and comprehensive, always rendering to our persecutors exactly what they are owed. Paul's exhortation also helps us trust the Lord when we find ourselves suffering unjust treatment at the hands of those who always seem to come out on top. No matter how successful they appear in this life, we know that God will deal with them in the end, and on that day, those who suffer for Christ will be exalted and will receive a great reward in heaven (Matt. 5:11–12).

Not only are we to refrain from taking vengeance on those who actively harm us, but we are to actively do good to them. The advantage of this is that such actions will "heap burning coals"

IV

DAY 68 & 69

FOR
FURTHER
STUDY

Deuteronomy
32:39-42;
Isaiah 34:8;
1 Thes-
salonians
4:3-6;
Hebrews
10:30-31

on the heads of our enemies (Rom. 12:20). Commentators do not agree on the meaning of this statement, which is actually a quote from Proverbs 25:21–22. The sense could be that our actions of kindness end up heaping more divine judgment on the heads of our enemies because the Lord will hold them accountable for treating us poorly and for the graver sin of opposing us when we do good to them. Or it could be that this text is telling us that our enemies will feel shame when we do good to them and perhaps cease their hostility or even be converted as the Spirit uses the shame to bring about repentance.

APPLICATION

What is your first inclination when people wrong you? Is it to seek vengeance on them, to do what you can to make them pay for what they have done? Or is your response immediately to pray for them, to ask God to bless them and bring them into His kingdom? When others hurt us, we must seek to do good to them insofar as we can. This does not mean that such things as lawsuits are always out of place. Nor does it mean that we should not report abuse and other criminal activity commit-ted against us and others to the governing authorities, for God uses them to punish evildoers (Rom. 13:4). Rather, it means that no matter what happens, we hope and pray for our enemies' salvation.

DAY 70

OVERCOMING EVIL WITH GOOD

ROMANS 12:21 "DO NOT BE OVERCOME BY EVIL, BUT OVER-COME EVIL WITH GOOD."

C ommentators on the book of Romans have pointed out the many conceptual similarities between Romans 12:14–21 and the teaching of Jesus in the Sermon on the Mount. Matthew 5:38–48, for example, covers many of the same themes that we have been reading about in our study of Paul's epistle to the Christians in Rome. During His earthly ministry, Jesus told us not to repay others in kind for the evil they do to us and that we should not simply endure suffering passively but actively love and serve our enemies.

These similarities are inevitable. After all, the Holy Spirit inspired Paul to write his letter to the Roman church, and since the Spirit and the Son are both fully God, the Word of God through Paul is ultimately the Word of the Son of God Himself. In any case, the theme of doing good to one's enemies is so important that the Apostle revisits it one more time in today's passage before he moves on to other aspects of the Christian life. Capping off his explanation of genuine love in the context of our interactions with other people, Paul tells us, "Do not be overcome by evil, but overcome evil with good" (Rom. 12:21).

The Apostle likely has several ideas in mind here. First, in doing good to those who hate us, we keep ourselves from being corrupted by the world and its way of doing things, and so we grow in our sanctification. We will be tempted to love the world and its sinful approach to reality, which is why John tells us not to love the world or the things of the world (1 John 2:15). As we do good when others hate us, we are not conformed to the pattern of this world; instead, we evidence the transformation that the Holy Spirit is working in us (Rom. 12:2).

Second, doing good to those who do evil against us can bring about the end of their evil. This does not always occur, but as we saw in Romans 12:20, people who have done wrong are often shamed when we do not repay them in kind, and they stop mistreating us. The Holy Spirit can even work in this to bring about the repentance and conversion of our foes. John Murray writes in his commentary *Romans*, "By well-doing we are to be the instruments of quenching the animosity and the ill-doing of those who persecute and maltreat us."

Finally, in doing good to those who hate us, we show forth the character of our Savior before the world. He loved those who hated Him so much that He gave up His life to save them. We cannot atone for sin, but we can imitate His love for His enemies by loving our foes, thereby pointing them to Christ Himself.

FOR FURTHER STUDY

1 Samuel 24; Proverbs 12:2-3; 14:19; 17:13; Matthew 5:38-42

IV

DAY 69 & 70

Let us note one more time that the high calling to love our enemies cannot be fulfilled in our own power. If we seek to do this through our own efforts, we will fail every time. But if we walk in the Spirit, God will give us a supernatural love for those who hate us, and we will find ourselves doing good even to our most dedicated enemies. May we pray for the Lord to give us this love, and may we encourage one another to walk in it.

DAY 71

THE PRIORITY OF LOVE

1 CORINTHIANS 13:1-3 "IF I GIVE AWAY ALL I HAVE, AND IF I DELIVER UP MY BODY TO BE BURNED, BUT HAVE NOT LOVE, I GAIN NOTHING" (V. 3).

J esus Himself says that love for God and love for neighbor are the most important commandments—on them the Law and the Prophets depend (Matt. 22:40). So that we might understand more fully the true meaning of love, we will spend a few days in 1 Corinthians, with devotionals based on Dr. R.C. Sproul's teaching series *Love.*

Any study of the biblical view of love must consider Paul's extensive exposition of the virtue in 1 Corinthians 13. This passage is a favorite text for many people and one of the most frequently read passages at weddings. Our familiarity with its contents, however, can blind us to how short we fall of this standard for love if we are not careful. The kind of love described in 1 Corinthians 13 is based on the love of our Creator Himself, which is never anything other than perfect. God's love is always kind, patient, truthful, and so forth, manifesting every quality that Paul ascribes to love in his epistle to the Corinthians. Moreover, the love of God demonstrates these characteristics flawlessly, while our attempts to love in this manner never measure up.

Why is our love imperfect? One reason is that we do not make love the priority it should be. Though it is the chief of all Christian virtues, we often ignore love and use our gifts destructively in the body of Christ, just as the Corinthians did (chs. 12–14). Envy consumes us, and we continually put ourselves ahead of others.

First Corinthians 13:1–3 tells us that though we might be extraordinarily gifted and have great theological understanding, we gain nothing if we have not love. Using the gifts of God without showing love to others only proves that we have forgotten the great Gift-giver, who is pure love (1 John 4:8). In so doing, all we have done is to replace the living God with a dead idol.

FOR FURTHER STUDY

Jeremiah 9:23-24; Hosea 4:1-3; Luke 10:25-37; 1 Corinthians 13:13

APPLICATION

Consider whether you make love a priority this day. Are you zealous to preach the gospel and defend truth because you like to win arguments, or are you motivated primarily by love for lost people? Is it more important to be right when you argue with your spouse, or do you seek to treat that person with love, no matter what is going on? If love is not a priority for you, repent this day and strive to make expressing love part of your nature.

`DAY 72`

NOT ENVIOUS OR BOASTFUL

1 CORINTHIANS 13:4 "LOVE DOES NOT ENVY OR BOAST."

N ear the beginning of his outline of love's characteristics in 1 Corinthians 13, Paul tells us that "love does not envy or boast" (v. 4). This is an interesting comment to make, but several considerations show us why the Apostle can make this statement.

Jonathan Edwards once defined envy as "a spirit of dissatisfaction and/or opposition to the prosperity and happiness of others." Therefore, an envious heart plainly violates Scripture's instruction on love. It reveals covetousness, that ungodly dissatisfaction with our possessions and/or circumstances and lust for that which belongs to others (Ex. 20:17). Envious people are unable to rejoice with those who rejoice (Rom. 12:15). When

IV

DAY 71 & 72

we are envious of others' blessings, we cannot take joy in their abundance, and we cannot truly love them or what our Father is doing in their lives.

Because our culture encourages and rewards envy, an improper love for whatever is not rightfully ours clearly violates the rule that we not be conformed to this world (Rom. 12:2). Politicians, celebrities, and advertisers exhort us implicitly and explicitly to be envious of those who seem to have more in the way of status, possessions, or power. Love that does not envy refuses to be envious of others who are blessed in ways that we are not. It is content with the Lord's provision in any circumstance.

Love also does not boast (1 Cor. 13:4). It is easy to become a cause for another person's stumbling when we are prideful and ostentatious, for such behavior can provoke others to envy. Creating stumbling blocks is not an act of love (Rom. 14). Those who manifest godly love do not make their own achievements into idols, and they do not build up their self-esteem at the expense of service to others.

Of course, having a negative self-image and manifesting godly love are not the same thing. We are made in God's image (Gen. 1:26–27), and caring for ourselves or realizing that we have dignity is not sinful. Actually, as God's image-bearers, we may view ourselves highly if we do not view ourselves more highly than is deserved (Rom. 12:3). Viewing ourselves accurately, Paul also says in Romans 12:3, requires a sober analysis of ourselves. Having a love that does not boast demands honesty about our weaknesses, respect for others, and reverent awe as we live before the face of Him whose image we bear.

FOR
FURTHER
STUDY

Psalms 8:3–
4; 31:23;
James 4:6

APPLICATION

Envy is an easy sin to hide because we can keep our mouths shut about what we are feeling in our hearts when we see others get blessings that we have been longing for. It is therefore important to be constantly considering our inward attitudes and confessing them before God and maybe even brothers or sisters in Christ whom we trust. Envy can lead to all manner of other sins, and so we must ever strive to keep it in check.

SELFLESS LOVE

1 CORINTHIANS 13:4-5 "LOVE IS PATIENT AND KIND; . . .
IT IS NOT ARROGANT OR RUDE. IT DOES NOT INSIST ON
ITS OWN WAY; IT IS NOT IRRITABLE OR RESENTFUL."

Having fallen in Adam, seeking to sit on the heavenly throne in place of our holy Creator, human beings have a bent toward selfishness (Gen. 3; Rom. 1:18–32). Before we knew Christ, we thought and acted as if we were the center of the universe, and after coming to faith we are still tempted to go back to our selfish ways. We often forget that love "does not insist on its own way" (1 Cor. 13:5). Love is not selfish.

True love is characterized by generosity, which seeks to give and not take for oneself, making it the very opposite of selfishness. Love means that we are willing to give our lives for the sake of others. This is how God has loved us, offering up His only begotten Son to die a shameful death under His wrath in order to save us (John 3:16).

Courtesy is one way that selflessness displays itself, since courteous people do not demand to be first in all things. Love is not rude (1 Cor. 13:5). It respects the rights and privileges of others, moving us to be polite and respectful to those around us. Whether we love others can be measured by how willing we are to be courteous to them, even if we must bend over backward to show respect. If we respect other people with our thoughts and language, and if we honor their time by keeping our appointments, we are showing a courteous love.

Besides evidencing generosity and courtesy, Paul also explains in 1 Corinthians 13:5 that Christian love "is not irritable or resentful." This cannot mean that loving people never get angry, for Scripture assumes that there are occasions on which we can be angry and yet not sin (Eph. 4:26). God Himself is perfect love, and yet He gets angry at sin. When Paul says that love is not irritable or resentful, he is talking about a love that keeps us from flying off the handle for any provocation.

IV

DAY 72 & 73

FOR
FURTHER
STUDY
___

Psalms
37:8;
103:8;
Proverbs
19:11;
1 Cor-
inthi-
ans 10:24;
James 3

Self-control, a fruit of the Spirit, is the antithesis to irritability (Gal. 5:22–23). Those who control their emotions instead of letting their emotions control them will not be irritable. This entails striving not to get angry over petty things or at situations over which we have little control. A love that is not irritable refuses to make everything a big deal. It encourages us to know our own weaknesses so that we can rightly assess our situation, maintain self-control, and respond appropriately to the circumstances we face. Love does not blow up in anger whenever things go awry.

APPLICATION

Do you struggle with a short temper? Are you quick to exaggerate things and make the worst out of any and all circumstances? The antidote to these things is remembering the patience of our Creator. He did not wipe us off the face of the earth the first time we broke His commands. He shows us patience today in calling us to repentance. If our great God has shown such love, how can we think that we can show any less toward others?

DAY 74

LOVE AND EVIL

1 CORINTHIANS 13:5-6 "IT DOES NOT REJOICE AT WRONG-DOING, BUT REJOICES WITH THE TRUTH" (V. 6).

U nfortunately, love is often defined in a shallow manner in today's culture and seen as something that overlooks the need to confront sin. Discipline at all levels is often ignored because holding people accountable is surely not the loving thing to do. God, however, never overlooks sin and wickedness, and since He is love (1 John 4:7–8), it is clear that true love is never afraid to face the reality of evil or make it less than what it really is. In today's passage, Paul helps us apply this idea practically, showing us how to view the evil that others do as well as the sin in our own hearts.

In the first place, love does not automatically assume the worst about other people when they wrong us. Love is not "resentful" (1 Cor. 13:5). Translations such as the New King James Version render the Greek for "resentful" as "thinks no evil," revealing that love does not quickly reach conclusions about the hearts of others. Real love makes us assume that other believers have the best of intentions when they have not repeatedly demonstrated otherwise. If we fail to assume the best of another Christian, we can impute evil motives where they are absent and grow resentful. Love never focuses on the wrongs that others do to us, recognizing that God alone knows the hearts of others.

There is an important qualification in all this, however. Love might think the best of others, but it is never naive. Discernment is required, and strong evidence of evil must prompt us to act properly in response (Matt. 10:16). But good discernment is possible only when we strive for impartiality in our evaluation of others.

Should we lack impartiality and assume the worst about others, we will probably violate love's demand that we never rejoice at wrongdoing (1 Cor. 13:6). Those who hastily impute ill motives to others invite gossip and slander. It comes as no surprise that our flesh loves to hear salacious stories and to retell another's sin or assumed motivations. Such acts evidence our rejoicing at wrongdoing, not what is good and holy.

In addition to being wary of gossip and slander, let us also be on guard against finding joy in the act of sin itself. The remaining presence of sin means that our hearts can become rebellious at a moment's notice, and Romans 1:26–32 warns us that the rebellious heart will approve of evil. Should we let down our guard against wickedness, we might grow increasingly attracted to evil and sear our consciences.

FOR FURTHER STUDY

Psalm 50; Proverbs 17:20; 21:23; James 1:19-21; Revelation 22:10-11

APPLICATION

Gossip and slander are two of the most overlooked sins in our day. We are quick to condemn sexual immorality, theft, and murder, but at the same time we often relish the opportunity to hear and tell stories about what others have said or done. When others are tempted to gossip in your presence, stand firm in the Spirit and suggest that the topic of conversation be changed to something more edifying.

IV

DAY 73 & 74

DAY 75

TRUTH AND HOPE

1 CORINTHIANS 13:6-7 "LOVE BEARS ALL THINGS, BELIEVES ALL THINGS, HOPES ALL THINGS, ENDURES ALL THINGS" (V. 7).

Signs of broken relationships dot the landscape of our culture. Talk-show hosts and other amateur counselors and gurus of the self-help movement are authorities to whom people flock as they look for the secrets of forming and maintaining good relationships and getting past griefs from years ago.

The sad reality of brokenness also drives people to denial about how bad things really are in our relationships. This happens even in the church as we do whatever it takes to avoid further disruption, even if it means exalting peace at the expense of the truth. But when we do this, we form superficial relationships, even allowing the root of bitterness to fester (Heb. 12:15).

Unfortunately, many Christians today are willing to tolerate gross sins in the church or to avoid sharing the gospel with unbelieving friends and family because they fear that a relationship might be lost. Yet while we should never break fellowship over minor issues or give unnecessary offense when we preach the gospel (Rom. 14:1–12; 1 Peter 3:14–16), we do no one a favor if we tolerate gross sin or never share the truth of Christ with others. Love always rejoices in the truth (1 Cor. 13:6), so it is impossible to love others if we deny sin or fail to tell unbelievers about the truth Himself.

First Corinthians 13:7 goes on to tell us that love "believes all things," which refers to the love we must have for that which the Almighty has revealed. Our God is the Lord of truth, and to love Him with our whole hearts and rejoice in the truth requires us to love His Word. Secondarily, "all things" refers to people in general. We are to be a trusting people who take others at their word when they have not given us reason to believe that they are lying. As with assuming the best about others, we need to be discerning, but we should always be quick to trust what other people say, especially our brothers and sisters in Christ.

Love also "hopes all things" (v. 7), and the term "hope" in Scripture refers not to a vain wish for something that may or may not happen but to a settled conviction that God will keep His Word. To "hope all things," then, is to be confident that we will see the Lord's immutable promises kept now or in the age to come.

FOR
FURTHER
STUDY

Psalms 42;
119:81;
Romans 5:1-
5; Gala-
tians 5:5;
Titus 1:2

APPLICATION

All of us have experienced betrayals in our lives wherein somebody did not keep a promise or otherwise violated our trust. When God calls us to be trusting people, He knows that many will betray us, but that does not give us license to refuse to trust anyone in the future. May we ask God to give us good discernment when it comes to trusting others and to equip us to be trustworthy people ourselves.

DAY 76

ENDURING LOVE

1 CORINTHIANS 13:7 "LOVE . . . ENDURES ALL THINGS."

Many people in our day have a shallow and superficial view of love that says that it is a mere feeling that is outside our control and can come and go as it pleases. If nothing else, 1 Corinthians 13 disabuses us of that notion. Indeed, we have seen that a true understanding of love, as God has revealed this virtue, realizes that love is a high calling, a demanding effort that must be put forward even when we do not feel like it. Love is no mere sentimental emotion. It actively works not to boast or show envy. Real love is selfless, and it refuses to rejoice in evil, choosing instead to seek out and proclaim the truth in all circumstances. This kind of love also has a sure hope for the future, believing the truth of the Lord's Word and taking what others say at face value until they prove themselves untrustworthy (vv. 1–7). True love, then, is a supernatural gift, because apart from our union with Christ, such love is impossible.

IV

DAY 75 & 76

In today's passage, we find the supernatural characteristics of Christian love reinforced when Paul explains that love will bear and endure all things (1 Cor. 13:7; see Gal. 6:2). Love perseveres in even the worst of circumstances, fulfilling the call of Peter and others to endure suffering of all kinds (1 Peter 2:20–21). But given the pain that this kind of suffering brings, such endurance is impossible without God's pouring love for Him—and thus for others—into our hearts through the Holy Spirit (Rom. 5:5).

Everyone who has ever suffered in a significant way from sickness or persecution understands that it is easy to let pain diminish our love for God. Tragedies can tempt us to doubt the Father's great love for us, but we should recall that the same Lord who poured love into our hearts also promises us a sure hope. His great love for us will be manifested in a new way at the return of Christ as He brings a new heaven and earth in which suffering will be nonexistent (Rev. 21:1–4). Reminding ourselves of this evidence of His love enables us to overcome any doubts about God's care as we suffer.

FOR
FURTHER
STUDY

Deuteron-
omy 31:6;
Psalm
100:5;
Proverbs
3:11-12;
Hebrews
11:32-40

Furthermore, our suffering proves God's love for us and gives us opportunities to share this love with others. Our suffering as Christians demonstrates His discipline for the sake of our sanctification, which is proof of God's love for His children (Heb. 12:7–11). Our pain also helps us relate better to other suffering people and minister in the name of Christ, thereby showing forth His love for them.

APPLICATION

To speak of suffering as a loving expression of God's discipline is not to say that there is always a one-to-one correlation between a specific sin that we have committed and our trial. Such a correlation may be true in some instances, but God's discipline is broader than just correcting us for specific sins. He is also teaching us to rely only on Him—to love Him absolutely even when everything may be falling apart around us.

GROWING UP IN LOVE

1 CORINTHIANS 13:11-13 "WHEN I WAS A CHILD, I SPOKE
LIKE A CHILD, I THOUGHT LIKE A CHILD, I REASONED
LIKE A CHILD. WHEN I BECAME A MAN, I GAVE UP CHILD-
ISH WAYS" (V. 11).

C hildren are used as examples in several passages in the New Testament, as Jesus and His Apostles exhort us to be childlike in several specific ways. Matthew 18:1–6, for example, says that we cannot enter the kingdom of God without becoming "like children" (v. 3). In 1 Corinthians 14:20, the Apostle Paul tells us how important it is for us to "be infants" with respect to doing evil.

These examples are metaphors, and clearly they are not designed to cover all aspects of the Christian life. Regrettably, Matthew 18:3 has frequently been taken in recent years to mean that we should not want to dig too deeply into the things of God. Instead of developing a concern to plumb the depths of Scripture, people have used Jesus' words to justify an ignorance of biblical doctrine and the distinctiveness of the Christian gospel. Such attitudes are childish, not childlike. That we must enter the kingdom like a child means that we must have the same dependent trust in God and all that He says in His Word that very young children have in what their parents do and say. It is not a justification for ignorance of His character and the doctrines taught in His Word. Moreover, to be infants with respect to evil refers to the skill that we are to have in knowing and doing what is wrong. As far as sin goes, we are to imitate young children, who are more open about their own shortcomings and who do not yet possess the finesse and expertise in the deeds of the kingdom of darkness.

Actually, Scripture repeatedly commands us to mature in our faith. First Corinthians 13:11, which exhorts us to abandon childish ways, is one passage that encourages such maturity. Our immature

IV

love should disturb us and move us to manifest the righteous, mature love that we see in this chapter. This requires us to put an emphasis on the fruit of the Spirit, one element of which is love (Gal. 5:22). Unlike the childish Corinthians, we are to pursue not the "flashy" gifts of the Spirit but maturity in doctrine and love.

FOR
FURTHER
STUDY

Psalm
143:9-12;
Hebrews
5:11-14

The New Testament calls us again and again to make slow, steady progress to maturity as we trust in Jesus (Heb. 12:1–2). Above all else, we are to seek after the kingdom of God and His righteousness (Matt. 6:33), and we can do this by seeking to manifest the righteous love of Christ described in 1 Corinthians 13.

APPLICATION

Knowledge of truth and the practice of love, as two of the chief indicators of Christian maturity, must both be emphasized in our walk with the Lord. Consistent study of the doctrines taught in the Bible is vital for our growth, and so is the love that demonstrates the attractiveness of the gospel. Ask yourself today if you emphasize truth more than love or love more than truth, and seek to bring both virtues into balance in your life.

DAY 78

CONTINUING BROTHERLY LOVE

HEBREWS 13:1 "LET BROTHERLY LOVE CONTINUE."

Orthodoxy, or "right belief," is an essential feature of biblical Christianity. We are saved through belief in the truth (John 14:6). Actions that please God are grounded in and informed by His truth. Scripture teaches this in many ways, including in the very structure of the biblical books themselves. For instance, the New Testament Epistles commonly place instructions for behavior after doctrinal teaching. Paul does this frequently in his letters. For example, Romans 1–11 explains doctrines, including justification, sanctification, glorification, and election. Romans 12–16 then explains how believers are to live in light of those great doctrines.

Hebrews follows a similar pattern. The first twelve chapters of the epistle do feature some practical applications, particularly the exhortation to persevere. Yet the bulk of the material focuses on the doctrine of the person and work of Christ. Practical instructions for Christian living are found mostly in Hebrews 13.

Chapter 13 begins by telling us to "let brotherly love continue" (v. 1). This is appropriate, for love is the chief of all Christian virtues (1 Cor. 13:13). Starting with love also makes sense given the focus of Hebrews on perseverance. Christians are in this race of faith together, and if we do not love one another, we will not spur one another on to love and good works (Heb. 10:24). Without such mutual encouragement, we are more likely to turn aside from following Jesus.

Brotherly love consists in more than just feeling. It displays itself in actions. In fact, true brotherly love is costly. We must give of our own time, choosing the needs of others over our own, in order to love people well. Christian love, in fact, is willing to pay the highest price of all. Loving others rightly means being willing to lay down our lives for them all the way to the point of death if we are so called. Jesus modeled this love perfectly for us, telling us that "greater love has no one than this, that someone lay down his life for his friends" (John 15:13) before He went on to die for the sake of His people.

Although we are sinners, those who are truly united to Christ by faith have a natural love for other believers implanted in them by the Holy Spirit. If one truly loves God, then one truly loves his brothers and sisters in Christ (1 John 4:20). A persistently unloving Christian does not exist. This does not mean that we will always love well, but it does mean that we will always seek to grow in love for other believers.

FOR FURTHER STUDY

Leviticus 19:18; John 13:34; Romans 12:10; 1 Thessalonians 4:9-10

APPLICATION

Do other Christians know that we love them? What evidences can we find in our lives that we love them? Since love is not a mere inward affection, it always bears fruit in action. Believers give of their time, money, and other resources in order to love one another well. If we are not sacrificing anything in order to love other believers, we may well not be loving them at all.

IV

DAY 77 & 78

HOSPITALITY TO ANGELS

HEBREWS 13:2 "DO NOT NEGLECT TO SHOW HOSPITALITY TO STRANGERS, FOR THEREBY SOME HAVE ENTERTAINED ANGELS UNAWARES."

L ove is the chief Christian virtue (1 Cor. 13:13), so it makes sense that the author of Hebrews begins his chapter of practical exhortation by commanding his audience to continue in brotherly love (Heb. 13:1). Much of what follows in Hebrews 13 actually reflects this exhortation to show love to others. We see this in Hebrews 13:2 and its call for us to show hospitality to strangers.

Ancient peoples prized hospitality. Traveling was not always safe, and inns were dangerous places to stay when one was on a journey. Christians relied particularly on the hospitality of strangers. As members of a new religious movement, Christians often had to endure rejection and inhospitable conduct from the Jews and pagans around them (Acts 17:1–9; 19:21–41). During His earthly ministry, Jesus had no place to lay His head (Matt. 8:20)—He had no permanent home. He depended on the hospitality of others. So a willingness to be hospitable to strangers was particularly important for the Christian community. Many Christians relied on the hospitality of "strangers" who were also professing believers in Jesus, men and women in the church whom they had never met before. It is a special display of Christian love to show hospitality to believers whom we do not know well.

The author of Hebrews adds further motivation for showing hospitality to strangers, explaining that in so doing, we may be entertaining angels without knowing it (Heb. 13:2). Most commentators believe that the author is thinking of Genesis 18, which records Abraham's visit with three men at the oaks of Mamre. These men turned out to be supernatural figures—angels—as Genesis 19 makes plain. Abraham went to great effort to be hospitable to these men, whose angelic nature was not evident to him, at least at first. In fact, later Jewish tradition came to view

Abraham as the example of hospitality par excellence because of his warm welcome of the angels.

A simple command to show hospitality in the Word of God is sufficient to make us understand the importance of being hospitable. That the strangers to whom we show kindness might even be angels makes us all the more willing to be hospitable to others. When we reject strangers, particularly professing Christian strangers, we might be rejecting supernatural agents of the Lord.

APPLICATION

A willingness to show hospitality insofar as we are able is an important part of obeying the Lord. It also helps us grow in the virtue of love. As we get to know Christian strangers better, we learn how to love them better and thus have more opportunities to show brotherly love. We should be going out of our way to be hospitable to fellow church members whom we do not yet know well and to show hospitality to traveling missionaries when they visit.

FOR
FURTHER
STUDY

Exodus
22:21;
Deuteron-
omy 10:19;
Romans
12:13;
1 Peter
4:9

DAY 80

REMEMBERING PRISONERS

HEBREWS 13:3 "REMEMBER THOSE WHO ARE IN PRISON, AS
THOUGH IN PRISON WITH THEM, AND THOSE WHO ARE MIS-
TREATED, SINCE YOU ALSO ARE IN THE BODY."

We know that many people in the original audience of Hebrews were considering apostasy because of the many exhortations in the letter to persevere (for example, Heb. 3:1–4:13; 10:19–39; 12:1–2). Yet the audience was not doing everything wrong. Proof for this is found in texts such as Hebrews 13:1, where the first readers of this epistle are told to "let brotherly love continue." To command that love continue assumes that the audience was loving one another when the epistle was written.

IV

DAY 79 & 80

Today's passage exhorts readers to "remember those who are in prison" (13:3), but the original audience seems to have been doing well in this area also. Hebrews 10:34, for instance, says that they had visited other believers in prison, at least in the days and months immediately after their conversion. The audience knew what to do; they just needed encouragement to continue doing so.

In any case, understanding life in ancient Roman prisons helps us see the importance of the command in Hebrews 13:3. In modern Western prisons, inmates for the most part receive food, clothing, and medical care from the government. It may not be the best food, clothing, and medical care, but by and large their basic needs do not go unmet. Ancient prisoners, however, did not receive such things from the government. They depended wholly on visiting family and friends to supply their physical needs. Prisoners who received no visitors went hungry in most cases. Ancient Christians in jail needed visits from fellow believers with food, drink, and other necessities.

Hebrews 13:3 speaks primarily of prisoners in jail because of their testimony to Jesus. Thus, believers cannot look the other way when Christians around the world are jailed simply for being believers. Yet the instruction of Hebrews 13:3 applies more broadly to visiting Christians in prison no matter the reason they are behind bars. Some people commit crimes while unconverted but later become believers while they are in prison. Others were true Christians when they broke the law, for it is possible for believers to commit grievous sins that have been criminalized by the secular authorities (for example, see 2 Sam. 11). We cannot forget these brothers or sisters either, no matter the gravity of their crimes. They need the support and encouragement of Christ's body to continue in repentance. Visiting Christian prisoners is one way to bear one another's burdens and fulfill the law of Christ (Gal. 6:2).

FOR
FURTHER
STUDY

Jere-
miah 37;
Matthew
25:31-46;
Acts 12:1-
5; 2 Timo-
thy 4:13

APPLICATION

Hebrews 13:3 reminds us of our responsibility regarding Christians who have been imprisoned for their faith, as well as those who have been mistreated for being believers. Often, such things take place far away, but that does not mean that we can forget them. We can pray for believers in prison around the world, give to organizations that advocate religious freedom, and more. As we are able, let us not forget believers who are in jail for their faith.

HONORING MARRIAGE

HEBREWS 13:4 "LET MARRIAGE BE HELD IN HONOR AMONG ALL, AND LET THE MARRIAGE BED BE UNDEFILED, FOR GOD WILL JUDGE THE SEXUALLY IMMORAL AND ADULTEROUS."

In the beginning, God established marriage so that man and woman would not be alone (Gen. 2:18–25). As the Lord's good gift, it is subject to His regulation for our well-being and for His glory. Moreover, since marriage constitutes one of society's foundational institutions, Scripture has much to say about marriage and the sexual relationship it sanctifies.

As the author of Hebrews continues his practical instruction for the church, he tells us that we are to "let marriage be held in honor among all, and let the marriage bed be undefiled" (Heb. 13:4). First, we note that this verse confirms marriage as an honorable and godly vocation for Christians. An unfortunate strain of unbiblical asceticism has led many people throughout church history to esteem the single life as inherently more virtuous than married life. Believers must take care not to embrace this understanding. Marriage is to be honored, and the church does well to promote and encourage the biblical view of marriage. To remain single is a noble calling, but it is not a more virtuous state than marriage. Moreover, honoring marriage requires us to obey the biblical standards for marriage and divorce, neither allowing divorce for frivolous reasons nor forbidding it where God permits it (Matt. 19:1–12; 1 Cor. 7:12–16).

Honoring marriage means doing what we can to keep the "marriage bed . . . undefiled" (Heb. 13:4). The immediate warning about God's judging the "sexually immoral and adulterous" in the same verse helps us understand what defiles the marriage

IV

DAY 80 & 81

bed. Fundamentally, the sexual unfaithfulness of a husband or wife defiles the marriage bed and dishonors it. God's moral law includes a prohibition of adultery (Ex. 20:14). Yet it is possible to defile the marriage bed—to use the sexual relationship in marriage wrongly—in ways beyond an actual physical affair. The term translated "sexually immoral" refers to a wide variety of sexual practices forbidden by God. Premarital sex, homosexuality, incest, bestiality, pedophilia, and pornography are all dishonoring to the Lord and to marriage (see Lev. 18). The marriage bed can also be defiled within marriage itself. Forcing a spouse into acts that are sexually degrading and demeaning of that spouse as the image of God defiles the marriage bed. Unjustifiably abstaining from sex is defiling as well (see Gen. 1:26–27; 1 Cor. 7:5). In their sexual relationship, as in all aspects of marriage, husbands and wives are to love one another.

FOR
FURTHER
STUDY

Proverbs 5;
Romans
13:13;
1 Corinthi-
ans 6:9-20;
1 Thessalo-
nians 4:3

APPLICATION

Our modern culture makes it difficult to keep the marriage bed undefiled. Yet with the help of the Holy Spirit, Christians can and must bring honor to the marriage bed. One way to keep from defiling the marriage bed is to endeavor to limit the avenues for committing sexual immorality. Let us strive not to put ourselves in situations where we are likely to commit sexual sin.

DAY 82

SEEKING CONTENTMENT

HEBREWS 13:5-6 "KEEP YOUR LIFE FREE FROM LOVE OF MONEY, AND BE CONTENT WITH WHAT YOU HAVE, FOR HE HAS SAID, 'I WILL NEVER LEAVE YOU NOR FORSAKE YOU.' SO WE CAN CONFIDENTLY SAY, 'THE LORD IS MY HELPER; I WILL NOT FEAR; WHAT CAN MAN DO TO ME?'"

nlike other law codes, the Ten Commandments address not just external acts of sin but the internal motivations that lead to those external acts. We see this most clearly in the tenth commandment, which prohibits covetousness (Ex. 20:17). Longing for something that we should not have and that properly belongs to someone else is the root of many, if not all, other sins. For instance, a woman does not commit adultery until she first sees and desires a man who is not her husband. A man does not steal unless he first sees and desires an object that is not his.

A sin such as adultery begins with coveting, so it is natural for the author of Hebrews to follow his teaching on adultery in Hebrews 13:4 with instruction on covetousness in verses 5–6: the love of money. Christians, we read, must be content with what they have, not greedy.

Let us note that the author prohibits covetousness, not riches. The Bible actually has many positive things to say about wealth, and believers such as Abraham were wealthy. In fact, sometimes the Lord rewards those who fear Him by giving them riches (Prov. 22:4). At the same time, God's Word also recognizes that money offers particular temptations. "The love of money is a root of all kinds of evils" (1 Tim. 6:10), for many people are willing to behave unethically if it will enrich them. Neither wealth nor poverty is inherently virtuous. One can be wealthy and not love money, and one can be poor and love money above all else.

Scripture frowns not on wealth as such but on the love of money, the pursuit of wealth as one's primary aim in life. People who love money sin because they are looking to money as their provider and not to the One who meets our needs and enables us to obtain wealth. Contentment with what we have is the sign of those who rely on God in all things. Now, contentment does not mean that it is always wrong to seek more than what we presently own. After all, God's Word commends wise invest-ment and taking actions to increase our wealth (for example, see Prov. 13:11). Instead, contentment means being happy with what we have even if our efforts to gain more prove unsuccessful. It means not being envious of those who are more financially successful than we are.

Love of money looks for security in things that cannot ulti-mately provide it. Those who do not love money strive to trust the Lord as the only source of their well-being (Heb. 13:5–6).

FOR
FURTHER
STUDY

Psalm
37:16;
Luke 16:13

IV

DAY 81 & 82

Augustine of Hippo comments on today's passage: "Put your hand in the purse in such a way that you release your heart from it." Christians may gain and enjoy their wealth, but they must always do so with a loose hand. Riches will never give us ultimate comfort and safety. Only God can do that. Loving money is foolish because it involves looking for something that money cannot provide—namely, eternal security and happiness.

DAY 83

RUNNING THE RACE OF FAITH

HEBREWS 12:1-2 "THEREFORE, SINCE WE ARE SUR-
ROUNDED BY SO GREAT A CLOUD OF WITNESSES, LET US
ALSO LAY ASIDE EVERY WEIGHT, AND SIN WHICH CLINGS
SO CLOSELY, AND LET US RUN WITH ENDURANCE THE
RACE THAT IS SET BEFORE US, LOOKING TO JESUS, THE
FOUNDER AND PERFECTER OF OUR FAITH, WHO FOR THE JOY
THAT WAS SET BEFORE HIM ENDURED THE CROSS, DESPIS-
ING THE SHAME, AND IS SEATED AT THE RIGHT HAND OF
THE THRONE OF GOD."

W ith the example of the Old Testament saints who persevered in faith despite not receiving in their lifetimes the fullness of God's promise, there is but one thing that we who live in the era of fulfillment in Christ can do: press on. Hebrews 11 has been building up to that very exhortation, and Hebrews 12:1–2 makes it explicit. Since we have the cloud of Old Testament witnesses, whose examples encourage us to persevere, we must "run with endurance the race that is set before us." We must trust Jesus until the very end, when we cross the finish line into the eternal joy of heaven.

Obviously, the author of Hebrews is using an athletic metaphor for the Christian life, much as Paul does in texts such as 1 Corinthians 9:24–27. The Christian life is like a race, with conversion the starting point and our entrance into glory the finish line. Finishing an ordinary race is no easy task. It takes effort to continue running. Various obstacles are in the way. We can get tripped up by our clothing. Our muscles tire and get sore. We may become so exhausted that we just want to give up. None of this surprises us when we run a footrace, so we should not be surprised that we sometimes find the race of faith difficult. It is supposed to take exertion to press on into glory. As the ancient biblical commentator and church father Jerome wrote: "God has entered us as contestants in a racecourse where it is our lot to be always striving. This place ... [is] an arena of struggle and of endurance."

Certainly, we should not grow discouraged. If we have been engrafted into Christ through faith in Him alone, we will certainly reach the finish line. No one who begins the race of faith fails to finish it. God glorifies all those whom He justifies (Rom. 8:29–30). Nevertheless, we do not finish the race without running the race. The sign that we have been united to Christ forever is that we do what the author of Hebrews tells us and put to death the sins that slow us down and tempt us to quit the race (Heb. 12:1).

We run the race, but we do not bring ourselves across the finish line. That job belongs to Jesus, who brings into His kingdom all those who look to Him in faith (v. 2). He went before us, believing that God would fulfill His promise to give Him a kingdom and a people, leaving for us an example of endurance. Let us continue trusting in Him this day and always as we run the race of faith.

FOR FURTHER STUDY

Psalm 123; Micah 7:7; Philippians 3:12-16; 2 Timothy 4:6-8

APPLICATION

Are you discouraged today, thinking that following Jesus is not worth it? Is sin wearing you down, tempting you to give in and to take your eyes off Christ? If so, now is the time to press on in the strength of the Spirit, trusting in God and His promises. Look to Jesus today, casting off your sin and asking Him to convince you that the prize at the end of the race is worth it. Only by continually looking to Jesus in faith will we cross into glory.

IV

DAY 82 & 83

CONSIDERING JESUS

HEBREWS 12:3-4 "CONSIDER HIM WHO ENDURED FROM SINNERS SUCH HOSTILITY AGAINST HIMSELF, SO THAT YOU MAY NOT GROW WEARY OR FAINTHEARTED. IN YOUR STRUGGLE AGAINST SIN YOU HAVE NOT YET RESISTED TO THE POINT OF SHEDDING YOUR BLOOD."

Hebrews 12:1–2 sets before us Jesus, to whom we must look in faith if we are to finish the race of the Christian life and pass into glory. Jesus is the premier example for believers because of His unwavering trust that His Father would give Him the joy that He set before His Son (v. 2). That joy consisted in His glorification, His exaltation as King of kings and Lord of lords (John 17:5; Eph. 1:20–21). We often forget, however, that we are His joy as well. Jesus' kingdom must have citizens, and those citizens are the people whom the Father has given to Him from all eternity (John 6:37). The joy for which our Savior trusted His Father is incomplete without the presence of His people. The wonder of that should inspire us to continue trusting Him until the end of our lives.

Continuing the call to look to Jesus as we run the race of faith, the author of Hebrews in today's passage tells us to consider the hostility Jesus faced in His mission so that we will "not grow weary or fainthearted" (Heb. 12:3). Here we are to remember that the Son of God willingly humbled Himself in His incarnation, taking on the form of a servant and subjecting Himself to all manner of hardship at the hands of evil people for the sake of our salvation (Phil. 2:5–11). If the eternal Lord of glory could do that, enduring suffering according to His human nature when He could in no way ever deserve it, how much more should we sinners be willing to do the same and like Jesus persevere when people hate us? John Calvin comments, "If the Son of God, whom it behooves all to adore, willingly underwent such severe conflicts, who of us should dare to refuse to submit with him to the same?"

In Hebrews 12:4, we get some insight into the situation of the original audience of Hebrews. The author notes that the first readers of his letter at that point had "not yet resisted to the point of shedding [their] blood." They had endured real suffering for their profession of faith, but things were not yet as bad as they can get on this side of glory. Christians struggle for a lifetime against sin and may even be tempted to fall away. It is an act of wickedness that we must resist. For some believers, successfully resisting it will mean a martyr's death when an evil government or other enemy compels them to choose between rejecting Christ for life in this world or following Him into physical death. Regardless of whether that specific choice ever comes to us, we must stand fast against apostasy.

APPLICATION

Jesus is the martyr par excellence, dying for His faithful witness to God and refusing to do anything but tell the truth of God even to those who hated Him. If we look to Him as our example, we must be willing to resist the calls to reject Him even to the point of shedding our blood to remain faithful. May the Holy Spirit give us the strength to do just that if we are ever called to do so.

FOR
FURTHER
STUDY

2 Chroni-
cles 24:20-
22; Mark
13:13

DAY 85

THE DISCIPLINE OF SONS

HEBREWS 12:5-10 "WE HAVE HAD EARTHLY FATHERS WHO DIS-
CIPLINED US AND WE RESPECTED THEM. SHALL WE NOT
MUCH MORE BE SUBJECT TO THE FATHER OF SPIRITS AND
LIVE? FOR THEY DISCIPLINED US FOR A SHORT TIME AS IT
SEEMED BEST TO THEM, BUT HE DISCIPLINES US FOR OUR
GOOD, THAT WE MAY SHARE HIS HOLINESS" (VV. 9-10).

IV

W e do not know completely the situation that the original audience of Hebrews found themselves in. The repeated calls to persevere in faith, the warnings about abandoning Christ, and the explanation of

DAY 84 & 85

the insufficiency of the old covenant throughout the book of Hebrews make us confident that the first readers of this book were being persecuted for their faith and were tempted to reject Jesus and return to the old covenant religion. Today's passage, however, does give us insight into the divine purpose behind their suffering. Hebrews 12:5–10 tells us quite plainly that God's discipline ultimately explained why the audience suffered as they were called to endure in faith.

Augustine, in his magisterial work *On the Trinity*, comments that in this passage, "discipline is spoken of in reference to those evils that anyone suffers for his sins in order that he may be corrected." That makes good sense of Hebrews 12:5–6, where the author of the epistle cites Proverbs 3:11–12 to make his argument. The passage in Proverbs has to do with correcting sin or error, so evidently the original audience of Hebrews faced persecution as divine discipline for transgression.

That is not to say, of course, that every episode of persecution or hardship that Christians face can be traced back to a specific sin. Scripture is clear in places such as the book of Job that not every trial falls on us because of a specific evil. But it is also clear in texts such as Deuteronomy 28 and 1 Corinthians 11:32 that some of the trouble we face is because of our sin. When we suffer, we should consider the possibility that we may be facing discipline for a specific sin, though in many (if not most) cases, we may not know the reason for our suffering.

In any case, the church father John Chrysostom comments, "Of necessity every righteous person must pass through affliction." That is exactly in line with today's passage, which says that the discipline of the Lord is a good thing inasmuch as it proves that we are His children and it makes us progress in holiness (Heb. 12:7–10). Often we believe that the discipline of the Lord proves that He does not love us, when exactly the opposite is true. Good fathers discipline their children so that they become responsible adults. Similarly, our heavenly Father disciplines us so that we become more like Him. If He did not discipline us, He would not be a loving Father.

FOR FURTHER STUDY

Deuteronomy 8:5; 2 Samuel 7:14-15; Psalm 94:12; Revelation 3:19

When we suffer the consequences of our sin or when we suffer for reasons that are totally unknown to us, we might think that God is against us. In both cases, however, the Lord is for us, and He is using our suffering to cultivate in us the holiness we must have in order to see the Lord (Heb. 12:14). Let us keep that in mind when we suffer, remembering that God is with us and is using our pain for our final good and His ultimate glory.

DAY 86

TEMPORARY PAIN, ENDURING FRUIT

HEBREWS 12:11 "FOR THE MOMENT ALL DISCIPLINE SEEMS PAINFUL RATHER THAN PLEASANT, BUT LATER IT YIELDS THE PEACEFUL FRUIT OF RIGHTEOUSNESS TO THOSE WHO HAVE BEEN TRAINED BY IT."

C ontinuing our look at the doctrine of discipline in the Christian life as explored in Hebrews 12, we understand that in many cases, we endure pain and suffering as the disciplinary consequences of our sin. That was certainly the case for the original audience of Hebrews, for God apparently allowed their persecution to show them the futility of their transgressions, which would have included entertaining thoughts of apostasy (vv. 1–7a). Not all suffering is due to our personal sins, however, and we can also understand discipline in a nonpunitive sense. For instance, there is the discipline of athletes who practice their sport, lift weights, work up their endurance, and so forth. In so doing, they become more adept and do better in their competitions. Scripture also speaks of discipline in this way (1 Cor. 9:24–27), and as we will see, even the author of Hebrews can use the metaphor in that way (Heb. 12:12).

In both cases, discipline proves God's love for us. Good earthly fathers do not allow their children to go undisciplined. A child who never faces discipline never attains maturity and has a distinct disadvantage when it comes to life in this fallen world. If even our good

IV

DAY 85 & 86

earthly fathers love us enough to discipline us for earthly success, how much more will our perfect heavenly Father discipline us for spiritual "success"? Because of divine discipline, we will share in God's holiness and thus see Him face-to-face in glory (vv. 7b–10, 14).

Today's passage makes the observation that we cannot understand the goodness of discipline if we do not consider the future. In the present, "all discipline seems painful rather than pleasant" (v. 11). Since we have a built-in aversion to pain, if we judge the value of our discipline merely by our present experience, we will think the discipline pointless and something to avoid. But just as earthly discipline produces maturity and equips us to do well, spiritual discipline from God the Father "later . . . yields the peaceful fruit of righteousness to those who have been trained by it" (v. 11). As John Calvin comments, "Chastisements cannot be estimated aright if judged according to what the flesh feels under them, and . . . therefore we must fix our eyes on the end."

John Owen notes that Hebrews 12:11 assures us that spiritual fruit will come in its due season. The Lord knows exactly how to discipline us so that we grow in spiritual maturity on His perfect schedule. God is sovereign even over our sanctification.

FOR
FURTHER
STUDY

Deuter-
onomy 11;
Job 5:17;
John 15:1-
17; James
3:13-18

APPLICATION

John Chrysostom writes, "Discipline is exercise, making the athlete strong and invincible in combats, irresistible in conflicts." Our discipline from the Lord does the same things for us spiritually, keeping us in the race so that we cross the finish line. Today let us take comfort that the Lord governs our sanctification and that His chastisement for our sin and His work through our practices of prayer and Bible study are conforming us to Christ in His perfect time.

DAY 87

A CALL FOR STRENGTH

HEBREWS 12:12-13 "THEREFORE LIFT YOUR DROOPING HANDS AND STRENGTHEN YOUR WEAK KNEES, AND MAKE STRAIGHT

PATHS FOR YOUR FEET, SO THAT WHAT IS LAME MAY NOT BE
PUT OUT OF JOINT BUT RATHER BE HEALED."

H ebrews 12 uses the metaphor of a footrace for the Christian life, calling us to run with endurance, setting our gaze on Jesus so that we cross the finish line (vv. 1–2). In the context of this metaphor, the notion of God's discipline of His people should be viewed both as His correction of sin and as His training us so that we can run the race with excellence (vv. 3–11). In today's passage, the author of Hebrews looks to our part in this training, reminding us that we have a role to play in our perseverance even though the Lord ultimately preserves us by His sovereign grace (see John 10:27–29; Phil. 2:12–13).

To finish a footrace, we must not let our hands droop and we must work so that our knees are strengthened and able to endure the wear and tear that running puts on them (Heb. 12:12). This athletic metaphor recalls the words of Isaiah 35:3: "Strengthen the weak hands, and make firm the feeble knees." In context, Isaiah refers to the coming of the Lord God to save His people, to ransom them from their enemies and from their exile (vv. 4, 10). This connection to the coming of the Lord reveals that lifting hands and strengthening weak knees, spiritually speaking, happens by remembering and believing the promises of God to save His people. This, of course, is in keeping with the commendations in Hebrews 11 of the men and women under the old covenant who trusted in the Lord, taking Him at His word of promise and looking for their final inheritance in glory. Spiritual strength comes not from our own resources but from the Lord, and that unfailing strength is the possession of those who believe in God's coming to save His people in the advent, ministry, death, resurrection, ascension, and return of the Son of God.

Hebrews 12:13 exhorts us to make "straight paths" for our feet. Runners have an easier time gathering and sustaining speed on straight paths than on circuitous racing routes that include many twists and turns. Since the path of a race is external to the runner, the focus here may be on looking for ways to arrange our external circumstances such that we are encouraged to keep on pressing

IV

DAY 86 & 87

FOR
FURTHER
STUDY
———
Psalm
10:17;
Ezekiel
34:16;
Acts 15:40-
41; 2 Tim-
othy 2:1

forward. Practically speaking, this could involve such things as coming up with a regular schedule of devotions, making it a priority to attend corporate worship, and building friendships with believers who will cheer us on in the Christian life.

APPLICATION

There is much that we can do to improve our running the race of faith that is the Christian life. The most important is making sure that we attend corporate worship regularly, week in and week out. Seeking to worship and rest on Sunday, scheduling our jobs so that we get Sundays off, and other such things make it easier for us not to miss worship and thus not to miss the means of grace.

DAY 88

OUR HEAVENLY HOME

JOHN 14:1-4 "IN MY FATHER'S HOUSE ARE MANY ROOMS. IF IT WERE NOT SO, WOULD I HAVE TOLD YOU THAT I GO TO PREPARE A PLACE FOR YOU? AND IF I GO AND PREPARE A PLACE FOR YOU, I WILL COME AGAIN AND WILL TAKE YOU TO MYSELF, THAT WHERE I AM YOU MAY BE ALSO" (VV. 2-3).

A s we have seen, Scripture tells us that there are only two ways to die. If we die in our sins—that is, without faith—we will be sent to the eternal suffering of the lake of fire (Rev. 20:11–15). If, on the other hand, we die in faith, we will be welcomed into the blessed presence of God Himself, where we will see Him face-to-face (John 3:16; 1 Cor. 13:12). Those who never rest in Christ alone for salvation will experience never-ending suffering, but suffering ends for the Christian at the moment of death. Then our communion with the Lord will be perfected, and we will enjoy His goodness forever.

At death, the believer goes to be with the Lord in heaven. Today's passage gives us some idea of what that home will be like. We will dwell in the Father's house (John 14:1–4). This is a homey, familial image that conveys warmth, love, and provision. Christ has promised—and He always keeps His Word—to bring us to heaven, where we will be perfectly secure and have no worries.

Interestingly, while the Christian concept of heaven has its own unique features, belief in an afterlife is not limited to Christianity. Except for atheists, who have always constituted a very small percentage of the world's population, people by and large affirm some kind of life after death. Some believe in reincarnation. Others believe in something like heaven. But it is almost impossible to find someone who denies that life after death is at least a possibility.

These various conceptions of the afterlife are all contradictory, so they cannot all be true. But the persistence of belief in some kind of life after death testifies that despite our best efforts, we cannot fully deny the revelation of God in creation. As Paul explains in Romans 1:18–3:20, all men know that there is a perfectly just Creator who will judge us according to the moral law written on our consciences. Yet we know that justice is not always done in this life. Some innocent people are convicted and some guilty people go free. This fact, plus the undeniable truth that the Judge of all the earth will do right (Gen. 18:25), provides the foundation for belief that justice not done in the here and now will be done on the other side of the grave. People might try to deny divine justice, but any concept of an afterlife where things are set right proves that we know that God will judge us and that we are guilty. Scripture insists that we will be declared righteous and able to withstand divine scrutiny after our deaths only if we trust in Christ alone (Rom. 3:21–26).

FOR FURTHER STUDY

Isaiah 51:6; Daniel 12:2; Philippians 3:20-21; Hebrews 6:13-20

APPLICATION

Without belief in what God has revealed, people will have a wrong conception of the afterlife. Nevertheless, belief in the afterlife proves that even people with wrong views of life beyond the grave cannot forget about divine justice. Though we are to be loving and kind to our neighbors regardless of whether they are believers in Christ, we must not hesitate to proclaim that a reckoning with God awaits us after death and that only in Jesus can we pass through it into eternal bliss.

IV

DAY 87 & 88

THE HOPE OF CHRIST'S RESURRECTION

1 CORINTHIANS 15:3-34 "BUT IN FACT CHRIST HAS BEEN
RAISED FROM THE DEAD, THE FIRSTFRUITS OF THOSE WHO
HAVE FALLEN ASLEEP" (V. 20).

We can have hope in our suffering only if there is an
afterlife—a place where all that is wrong with this
world will be set right. Much of the suffering that we
endure is unjust. People slander us, besmirching our good names
without just cause. Others are envious of us and thus act with
hatred toward us. In this world, the righteous do not always win.
Often, the wicked prosper (Ps. 73:3). If our suffering is to have any
meaning and purpose, this cannot last forever. Without a Judge
to perfectly dispense rewards for righteousness and punishments
for evil, suffering for righteousness' sake is in vain. There is no
transcendent good or evil. Everything is permissible because no
one will ever be finally held to account.

In our postmodern context, many people might say that there
is no such thing as absolute good or absolute evil, but precious
few really believe that. People still cry out for justice to be done.
Almost no one lives life without any restraint at all. Individuals
from all kinds of backgrounds say that "everything happens for
a reason." Belief in right and wrong endures in practice if not in
principle.

Yet the persistence of such a belief is not evidence in itself
that an afterlife exists and that God will judge wickedness and
reward holiness. Moreover, mere belief that there is a deity does
not answer the question as to which god is the true one. Thankfully, the Apostle Paul gives us evidence both for the afterlife and
that God will judge the world in righteousness. First Corinthians
15:3–34 lays out an argument that shows how the resurrection of
Jesus confirms that there will be a final resurrection of the dead
and that the Lord will judge the world in perfect righteousness.
Everything hangs on Jesus' being raised from the dead. It is not
that there might be another viable contender for the one true

God if Jesus has not been raised. No, if Jesus has not been resurrected, there is no divine Judge and no divine judgment. So we might as well do whatever we please (v. 32). Yet it is certain that Christ has been raised from the dead. The Old Testament points to Him, and the witnesses to His rising from the dead testify to the veracity of His resurrection (vv. 3–8). Our faith that there is a God who gives meaning to all our suffering because He will sit in judgment is no mere fancy. It is supported by solid evidences.

APPLICATION

There are many books that present the historical evidence for the resurrection of Christ, and it can be helpful to be aware of the convincing case that Jesus rose from the dead. If we are confident of the resurrection, we will be assured that there is a day of judgment to come when our suffering will be vindicated. As we are able, let us study so as to grow in our conviction of the resurrection and to bear witness to the truth of Christ.

FOR FURTHER STUDY

Psalm 16:9-10; Jeremiah 23:5; Ezekiel 37:25; Luke 24

DAY 90

OUR JOY TO COME

REVELATION 21:1-27 "BEHOLD, THE DWELLING PLACE OF GOD IS WITH MAN. . . . HE WILL WIPE AWAY EVERY TEAR FROM THEIR EYES, AND DEATH SHALL BE NO MORE, NEITHER SHALL THERE BE MOURNING, NOR CRYING, NOR PAIN ANYMORE, FOR THE FORMER THINGS HAVE PASSED AWAY" (VV. 3-4).

Heaven, that place where we will see God face-to-face and enjoy Him forever, has been the focus of our last few devotionals. We have also seen how knowing that the Lord will judge all people gives us hope in the midst of our suffering. Much of our study has assumed the existence of heaven as part of what theologians call the *intermediate state*. We certainly go to be with the Lord in heaven if we die in faith before Christ returns (2 Cor. 5:6–8), but our presence in heaven before Jesus' second advent is an intermediate state of our existence

IV

DAY 89 & 90

after death, not the final or ultimate state that we will enjoy. In other words, the spiritual disembodied existence that we will enjoy in heaven before Christ returns will come to an end and another state will take its place. As Scripture teaches us in many places, the resurrection of the dead will happen. Heaven will come down to earth, and we will have physical bodies and live in a perfected creation.

One of the most important passages on the new heaven and earth is Revelation 21, which describes this new creation. We should greatly look forward to the bliss we will experience there. We will have a foretaste of it in the intermediate state, but its fullness will be ours only when Christ comes to consummate His kingdom. At that point, we will enjoy the unmediated presence of God, for the whole universe will be His temple (vv. 3–4). This will be possible because there will be a new heaven and a new earth in which righteousness dwells (v. 1; 2 Peter 3:13).

This perfect new creation will be free from all sadness. There will be no more tears, for God will have wiped them all away. Death, disease, emotional pain, sin—all the things that bring us so much suffering will pass away. We will bear the image of God with utter clarity, and there will be no strife. Though there will be continuity between this present creation and the one to come—God will not wipe everything out but will resurrect and renew all things—there will also be significant discontinuity, for God's dwelling among us means that we will have perfect communion with Him (Rev. 21:2–4).

FOR
FURTHER
STUDY

Isaiah
65:17;
2 Peter
3:13

Our final home will be both beautiful and grand (vv. 9–21), and we will dwell in perfect light because the Lord's glory will illumine His creation. God will be our lamp, and we will need no sun, no moon, no candles, no other source of light. We will be content to see His beauty and rejoice that we dwell in such incredible glory (vv. 22–27).

APPLICATION

It might be hard to imagine, but being able to see our Lord face-to-face is going to be the most incredible sight we could ever experience. We will be so enthralled with His beauty that we will never tire of gazing upon Him in His glory. We will never be bored in learning more about our infinite Creator. We will always rejoice in His perfect love. Our suffering will have been worth it because it will have led to the vision of God's full beauty and glory.

IV

DAY 90

ABOUT LIGONIER MINISTRIES

Ligonier Ministries is an international Christian discipleship organization founded by Dr. R.C. Sproul in 1971 to proclaim, teach, and defend the holiness of God in all its fullness to as many people as possible. Dr. Sproul dedicated his life to helping people grow in their knowledge of God and His holiness, and our desire is to support the church of Jesus Christ by helping Christians know what they believe, why they believe it, how to live it, and how to share it. If you would like to learn more about Ligonier or discover more resources like this one, please visit Ligonier.org.